JAPANESE CULTURE

THE EAST-WEST CENTER—formally known as "The Center for Cultural and Technical Interchange Between East and West"—was established in Hawaii by the United States Congress in 1960. As a national educational institution in cooperation with the University of Hawaii, the Center has the mandated goal "to promote better relations and understanding between the United States and the Nations of Asia and the Pacific through cooperative study, training, and research."

Each year about 2,000 men and women from the United States and some 40 countries and territories of Asia and the Pacific area work and study together with a multinational East-West Center staff in wide-ranging programs dealing with problems of mutual East-West concern. Participants are supported by federal scholarships and grants supplemented in some fields by contributions from Asian/Pacific governments and private foundations.

Center programs are conducted by the East-West Communication Institute, the East-West Culture Learning Institute, the East-West Food Institute, the East-West Population Institute, and the East-West Technology and Development Institute. Open Grants are awarded to provide scope for educational and research innovation, including a program in humanities and the arts.

East-West Center Books are published by The University Press of Hawaii to further the Center's aims and programs.

JAPANESE CULTURE
A Study of Origins and Characteristics

by EIICHIRO ISHIDA, 1903-68

translated by TERUKO KACHI

AN EAST-WEST CENTER BOOK
The University Press of Hawaii
Honolulu

© University of Tokyo Press, 1974
Published in the United States of America by The University
Press of Hawaii

ISBN 0-8248-0325-6

Library of Congress Catalog Card Number 73-92494

Printed in Japan

Contents

Translator's Preface

Professor Eiichiro Ishida (1903–68), a distinguished scholar of ethnology and cultural anthropology, conducted field research in Japan, continental Asia, and South America. He held a doctorate from the University of Tokyo and was a member of the American Anthropological Association, simultaneously serving as president or director of several Japanese scholarly societies. His books and monographs on ethnology, cultural anthropology, and Japanese cultural history, which reveal his wide range of interests, have recently been published in a multi-volumed collected works.

The Japanese edition of *Japanese Culture (Nihon bunka ron)*, published in 1968, was based on public memorial lectures given at Seijō University, Tokyo, in 1965, in honor of the late Kunio Yanagita, the founding father of Japanese folklore studies. Although these lectures were published posthumously without benefit of the author's final revision, and their scope does not do full justice to the breadth of Professor Ishida's scholarship, they explore the sources of Japanese culture, with the insights gained from the many-faceted research and thoughts of the writer. The book thus makes a unique contribution to an understanding of comparative culture, developing further the theories of the philosopher

Tetsuro Watsuji, as presented in his influential *Fūdo* [Climate and culture], first published in 1935, and serves also as an introduction to the various studies in the social sciences pursued in postwar Japan. The activities of Japanese social scientists, stimulated by the liberal atmosphere of the years since 1945, continue to bear fruit in publications which, unfortunately, have not been readily accessible to Western scholars because of the language barrier. In his book, Professor Ishida has revealed to the reader the tip of an iceberg, as it were. In order to assist the reader in his own explorations, I have compiled the footnotes, a selective bibliography, and chronologies of Chinese and Japanese history. For those who wish to read the works of Professor Ishida in Japanese, there is a separate bibliography of his representative studies. It is hoped that *Japanese Culture* will be of use in English-speaking colleges and universities which offer courses in East Asian studies.

Professor Ishida was a member of the Planning Committee for the establishment of the Department of International and Cultural Studies at Tsuda College in 1967. It is due to his advice that the curriculum of the department thus established includes a basic required course on Japanese society and culture, and the first lectures were to have been given by Professor Ishida himself. The present translation is a small tribute to the memory of a humane scholar of international stature whose sudden death in 1968 brought deprivation to Japanese social science and sorrow to those who knew him as an enthusiastic teacher and colleague, and a wise counselor.

I would like to offer my sincere appreciation and gratitude to Professor Fujio Ikado of Tsuda College for his kindness and guidance; to Mr. Shigeo Minowa and Mrs. Elizabeth Kodama of the University of Tokyo Press for their patience and advice; to the following colleagues and friends for information on specific points: Professors Se-kai Koh,

Akiko Ueda, and Yoshiie Yoda, Mrs. Nobuko
Sando, Mr. Rex Longden, and Professor George
Akita; and to Mr. Yukio Fujino, librarian of the
International House of Japan Library, and his staff
for numerous courtesies.

JAPANESE CULTURE

Introduction: Culture and Peoples

The Theme of Japanese Cultural Studies

I belong to the generation of scholars who knew the late Kunio Yanagita[1] and greatly benefited from his research long before World War II, though I cannot claim that I have made an intensive study of the scholarly field of Japanese folklore which he established. My own field of research has been slightly different, and I do not yet feel fully prepared to discuss Japanese culture. However, I appreciate the opportunity to express my present views on this subject.

I have conducted research on Japanese culture at the Research Institute for Japanese Culture, Tōhoku University, and have also lectured on this theme there. In my opinion, the purpose of the study of Japanese folklore is to understand Japanese culture. For the Japanese people, this discipline provides a medium for the pursuit of self-knowledge. The discipline therefore covers aspects of our traditional culture that are still living today, as well as our cultural traits, racial characteristics, and national character. The study of Japanese folklore is in fact the study of Japanese culture.

Since my studies have been in another, related field, I would like to explain my own attitude toward the study of folklore, pointing out the future problems facing this discipline and the questions that I have concerning its approach and direction. The German philosopher Karl Löwith,[2] who once

1. 1875–1962. Founder of the scientific study of folklore in Japan. His work as a government official in agriculture brought him in touch with farmers and aroused his interest in folk culture. He recorded various village customs and tales, and in 1950 he made an extensive classification of the latter in his *Nihon densetsu meii* [Index of Japanese legends]. He wrote voluminously on the results of his studies, founded one periodical and edited another in the field of folk culture, and in 1947 established an institute for research on folklore. He has also conducted research on Japanese dialects. His collected research works have been published in Japanese, but very few of his studies have been translated into English. This influential scholar, therefore, is not well known outside Japan.

2. 1897–1973. Lecturer at Marburg University, 1928–36; lecturer at Tōhoku University, Japan, 1936–41; residence in the United States. After 1952 Löwith taught at Heidelberg University. He wrote on Weber, Marx, Kierkegaard, and Nietzsche.

lectured at Tōhoku University, commented on the differences between East and West in the following passage:

> The ancient Greeks became aware of themselves as a unique people when they realized their difference from "other peoples," that is, the neighboring races in the Near East. Since we customarily tend to become aware of our own distinctive characteristics and way of life when we differentiate ourselves from others, men lacking contact with alien peoples do not know their own character, their own basic nature. . . .
>
> The contrast based upon distinctions does not imply the resolution of differences. On the other hand, it may lead to confrontation. Comparison of oneself with others invites self-criticism. Blindness to oneself springs from ignorance of the ways of others.

This is also a problem that concerns the study of Japanese folklore and Japanese culture. Yanagita's scholarship developed during the Meiji, Taishō, and Shōwa eras, [3] when modernization and Japan's confrontation with the West took place. In all probability it was this confrontation with the West that provided the incentive for the unfolding of this scholarly discipline, as Yanagita sought to realize this self-awareness against the surging tides of modernization. We, in turn, need to examine the future direction of the study of Japanese culture through the study of Japanese folklore.

My own research, however, has been directed largely to scenes other than Japan. Since I was born in the Meiji period, from early years I perceived the existence of the West as a vast alien factor, as I wrote in Tōzai-shō [Essays on East and West]. I have returned to my initial interest in Japanese culture as a consequence of my reflections on this,

3. The names of the "year periods" (i.e., reigns) of the last three emperors, including the present emperor, which cover the period of Japan's modernization: Meiji, 1868–1912; Taishō, 1912–26; Shōwa, 1926 to the present. The practice of counting time by year periods was introduced to Japan from China in the seventh century.

and through my constant awareness of the West as well as my study there.

The Formation of a People's Individuality

I have always cherished a strong interest in cultural history, especially in its beginnings in ancient times. Therefore, the present study of Japanese culture encompasses issues touching upon the origins of the Japanese culture and people, and the formation of the state, which may give readers the impression that I am merely retracing the early history of Japan. However, it is the Japanese culture of today that concerns me. I hope to throw light upon its nature and its patterns by clarifying the questions of when, where, and how it was formed.

We can consider the problem of when the basic characteristics, the leitmotif, of a culture were formed by comparing them with the personality of an individual. A great many psychologists and anthropologists hold the view that the core of the personality of the individual is formed during childhood, and that this core personality endures until the death of the individual. My own experiences lead me to believe that there is much to be said for this theory. Children tend to overestimate the differences that separate them from grown-ups, and to stand in awe of grown-ups, with their greater experience of life. This attitude persists into adolescence. However, after middle age, with the accumulation of more than half a century of life's experiences, it becomes apparent that the basic personality formed in childhood has not changed at all—even in elderly men past the age of sixty. Sometimes one recalls how a friend who has an appreciation of leisure and is slow to anger was like this even in his childhood; on the other hand, a short-tempered man may develop some restraint, but his basic trait does not change with age.

If we were to apply this model to the culture of a people, might we not come to understand the formation of a people's individuality—the fundamental traits that correspond to the core personality of the individual—by returning to the circumstances of the period in which this people was formed as a distinct group?

Bearing this in mind, I have studied Japanese culture and have considered how and when the two following factors can be related: first, the origins of the Japanese; second, the Japanese people as they are today, with their distinctive cultural traits. As a general hypothesis, I am inclined to propose the existence of a continuous pattern that does not easily change, and I hope to be able to support this hypothesis of continuity by presenting evidence of certain significant trends in Japanese history. At present, my effort may result only in pointing out the basic issues, but I trust this will be of some value in itself. Possibly in ten or twenty years' time, as younger scholars pursue further research on these issues, they may find solutions to the questions that puzzle me today.

1. Who Are the Japanese?

Common and Distinctive Aspects of Culture

I would like to begin by considering some familiar problems that were raised in a recent series of newspaper articles. A few years ago, the evening edition of the *Asahi* ran a series entitled "Arabia yūboku-min" [The Arabian nomadic peoples]. These articles were written by Shōichi Honda, [1] who had gone with a cameraman to live first among the Canadian Eskimos, and then among the primitive mountain tribes called Moni and Dani, living in the New Guinea Highlands. His observations were later published as two books, *Kanada Eskimo* [The Canadian Eskimos] and *Nyū Ginia kōchi-jin* [The New Guinea Highland peoples], both extremely interesting and replete with vivid narrations of the author's experiences and observations. The two books are now available in one volume, entitled *Kyokugen no minzoku* [Peoples living in extreme climatic conditions].

The peoples he described are alive and human. The Eskimos who hunt in the North Pole and the tribes who pursue a primitive form of agriculture in the remote interior of New Guinea are people like ourselves, and, as we read his accounts, we become intimately acquainted with them. The same author has recently gone to live among the Arabian nomads and has now given us a detailed report of his experiences there. What relation can we find

1. 1933—. Travel writer and reporter for the *Asahi*, one of Japan's leading daily newspapers.

between these reports and our present study of
Japanese culture?

Honda commented on his feeling of congeniality
with the Canadian Eskimos and the New Guinea
Highland peoples, which sprang from a strong
consciousness of a common humanity shared by
all men, whether they live in primitive or civilized
conditions. Then, on his third expedition, he entered a community of Arabian nomads. These
Arabians, whose history dates back to ancient times,
have developed an extremely complicated etiquette
as part of their social mores. They take turns defer-
ring to each other when they sit together, and they
follow refined rules of hospitality. It was their
ancestors who built the mighty empire of the
Saracens with its impressive civilization. Yet once
Honda had entered the world of the nomadic
Bedouins, who are also Arabian, he discovered
how different men could be and became keenly
aware of the difficulty of understanding a people
with a history so different from that of the
Japanese.

Now, in this I discovered one clue to the study
of Japanese culture that I should like to discuss. For
example, Honda describes how, at a hotel in Riyadh,
he was given the wrong key to his room, so he went
back to the front desk and said, "Well, I'm afraid
I can't get in with this," smiling a little with the
typical Japanese concern to avoid blaming others.
To his astonishment, the answer was the unexpected
retort, "That's because you gave me the wrong
number." In Japan, the episode would have ended
with the clerk remarking, "I'm sorry," or "Please
pardon me," but in Arabia the immediate response
was an excuse: "That's because you gave me the
wrong number."

Although this incident amazed him, Honda had
in fact already experienced during his contacts with
the Bedouins the grasping nature of nomadic peoples, which arises from a kind of predatory culture,

an alien culture developed under the harsh tooth-and-nail conditions of the desert, so that, for example, a debt contracted was seldom repaid, any number of excuses being made to avoid the responsibility. The above case also struck him as being typical of the Bedouin.

Tetsuro Watsuji's famous work *Fūdo* [Climate and culture] describes the culture of this literally "dry" desert people as being characterized by a "dryness of thinking."[2]

Shōichi Honda's Findings

The following observations of Honda are relevant here.

Admitting one's mistakes is equivalent to unconditional surrender. According to the Arabian proverb "No human being can be trusted," a man has no right to protest, no matter what treatment he receives.

When the Mongols invaded territory close to Arabia, they declared they would save all who surrendered unconditionally; then they massacred the enemy and held a banquet upon boards placed on top of the corpses. I imagine they too were nomadic races.

(The Mongols were, in fact, a nomadic people.)

Even if a man fails in some venture, he must never admit this. Suppose he broke a hundred-yen plate and admitted this; a Bedouin might demand a thousand-yen compensation. That's why an Arab who has broken a plate would say, "The plate was fated to break today. It had nothing to do with my intentions."

Let us imagine the reverse situation. A Japanese who broke a plate would certainly say immediately, "I'm very sorry," and a conscien-

2. 1889–1960. An original thinker who attempted to combine the Eastern moral spirit with Western ethical ideas, Watsuji was a professor of ethics at Kyoto University and the University of Tokyo. His early writings on Nietzsche and Kierkegaard prepared the way for the later introduction of existentialism into Japan. He then turned to the study of various aspects of Japanese culture, including Buddhism, and used the results of a positivist historical approach in his research on Japanese cultural history. His major works are on ethics, and his study of climate and its effects on peoples is the expression of an original theory of cultural history closely related to his thinking on community. He saw man as having a dual existence as both an individual and a social being, and man's ultimate nature he felt to be "absolute nothingness," according to Buddhist thought, which could be expressed in the mutual relations of men in community from the family to the state. Only one of his works, *Fūdo*, has been translated into English: *Climate and Culture*, translated by Geoffrey Bownas (Tokyo: Hokuseido Press, 1971).

tious person might add, "It was my fault." Such an attitude is a virtue, but not one universally accepted. The Arabians act in quite the opposite manner. In India, the views held may be similar to those of the Arabians, and in France they might say, "An Italian plate would have been more durable."

Since my own experience was limited, I collected other examples of such "reactions to faults" from many friends and acquaintances, in Japan and elsewhere, and I discovered something important. Among the major countries, there seemed to be few with the custom of apologizing immediately upon breaking a plate. There were practically none where people would be so good-natured as to say, "It was my fault." If one put Arabia and Japan at opposite poles, European countries would prove to be closer to Arabia than to the center. Even in China, Japan's nextdoor neighbor, I could find few if any cases of immediate apologies. However, Europeans apologize more casually than Japanese in trivial matters which do not involve compensation (such as accidentally touching a person or making a bodily noise through indigestion). This sort of apology is just a custom (like the Bedouin's "kindness").

But I do know of cases that are certainly close to those of the Japanese. These are the customs of the Eskimos and the Moni of New Guinea. If they accidentally tore my notes, or smudged the lens of my camera with dirt, the Moni invariably apologized by saying, "Amakane [I am sorry]." Reviewing these cases, we reach a general conclusion:

"The more a country has experienced invasions from other peoples, the less likely its people are to admit their faults."

The Japanese, the Eskimos, and the Moni, who have had comparatively few tragic contacts with other peoples, are exceptionally good-natured.

The fundamental outlook of the Bedouin, or, in fact, the Arab, is far more universally shared than that of the Japanese. We may consider our people's character closer to that of the peoples of New Guinea than to Arabia, Europe, or China. When I spoke about this on my return to Professor Sasuke Nakao[3] of Osaka Metropolitan University, one of the most widely traveled of Japanese, he said, "I suppose Japan is the world's last unknown frontier."

Shortly after our return, a letter to the *Asahi* was published. It was about not taking things lying down any more, and it had been written as a consequence of the unfortunate experience of the writer, who apologized after being involved in a minor accident for which he had not been responsible at all. If an Arab had read this letter, he would have been dumbfounded at this truly Japanese phenomenon. In a similar situation, even if they had been a hundred percent in the wrong, they would invariably have declared, "It's a hundred percent your responsibility."

This is the conclusion of Honda's story.

The National Character of the Japanese and Other Peoples

I have cited his article because, speaking from my own experience, I think that in general these observations are justified. For instance, a Japanese who was driving a car in America collided with another car in circumstances in which the responsibility did not lie with either driver. Yet, inadvertently, he said, "Excuse me," and the remark was held as evidence that he had admitted his responsibility; he lost his case in court and was fined.

3. 1916—. A botanist well known for his ecological studies of Japanese culture.

In another Western country, I heard a similar story from a Japanese. A woman driver bumped into his car. Though it was clearly her fault, the first words she spoke were, "It was not my fault." The Japanese told me he had felt angry at this thick-skinned reaction, a prompt denial of responsibility.

In Japan today, the attitudes of young drivers have changed a good deal. Yet how many would claim instantaneously that it was not their fault when they were clearly in the wrong in a collision? I have not had any contact with the Bedouins, but I have lived in China, in Europe, and in America. I would say from my own experience that the Western cultural pattern of behavior is more widespread than the Japanese pattern. It is held to be justifiable for a man to protect his own position, if it is clear that otherwise he would suffer a defeat.

Of course, Western culture is far more refined than that of the Bedouin, and, in some respects, much more than that of the Japanese. People say "excuse me" automatically even when they cough a little during a conversation. Unless there is a specific conflict of interests, they are extremely kind to other people, and close friendships formed between individuals last a lifetime.

Since we are all human beings, naturally we share many common characteristics. However, a Japanese would sense a greater strictness in daily life among Europeans, since in that context acknowledging fault would mean accepting the consequences without question.

It is said that, in the fierce competition of business negotiations with Europeans, the average Japanese businessman, unable to stand up to the Europeans' toughness, is completely overwhelmed. He is reduced either to what appears to be obsequiousness, or to an unnecessary aggressiveness. This is only one case in point, but I would like to consider the Japanese through comparison with other peoples. In other words, I hope to contrast the distinctive traits of Japanese culture and Japanese national character with those of other peoples.

Is a Classification according to Racial Characteristics Possible?

We start with the problem of who the Japanese are. In discussing the Japanese, what is our criterion for defining this race? Obviously, the concept of a "Japanese people" implies the existence of other human beings who are not Japanese. If the whole of mankind consisted solely of the Japanese, then our present concept of the Japanese would not exist. For when we use such words as the Japanese or the Japanese race, it is because we think of the existence of a separate group of human beings whom we can compare with other human beings.

Then what criterion can be used to distinguish one from the other? This question appears to be one of simple common sense; however, it is difficult to answer. For instance, we might think it easy to tell a Japanese from his facial features, but actually this is not the case. I happened to travel in the Republic of Korea recently, and on a train going from Seoul to Kyongju, the former capital of the ancient kingdom of Silla near the coast of the Japan Sea, I found myself in a carriage for seventy passengers, almost all of whom were Koreans. As I looked at them I began to wonder what percentage of them would look distinctly non-Japanese, supposing the train were running somewhere in Japan. Of course, as I made my observations, I made a deliberate effort to detach myself entirely from the consciousness that I was in a foreign country, and I concluded that the non-Japanese faces amounted to less than 10 percent.

Suppose we had made the same observations in Japan in a train full of Japanese. If we had divested ourselves completely of our preconceptions about the Japanese and had concentrated on whether or not the passengers looked Japanese, I think we would have discovered several faces that looked Korean or Chinese.

Anthropologists use physical traits in classifying different races (standards of measurement such as facial features, the shape of the skull, the color and texture of the hair, skin color, characteristics of the color of the eyes), but the difficulties of defining the limits make many of them skeptical about the validity of such categories. Some scholars, in fact, hold that there is no such thing as race. One may question this assumption, saying that the differences between the white man and the Negro surely constitute "race"—to which the answer would be that it is easy to distinguish the two extremes, but that there are any number of gradations of mulattoes; even in America, a man who is indistinguishable in looks from a white man may be socially discriminated against as a black man.

The Formation of a People and the Unification of a State

I do not deny that race exists, but if the concept of "race" and the concept of a "people" are not identical, what criterion should we use to distinguish a people? In addition, there is also the word "nation," denoting a people who form a state and who possess the nationality of that state. Since it is true that those of Japanese nationality are Japanese, we find that the people of a certain "nationality," using this legal term, cannot be divorced from the political entity called a nation.

However, history and common sense show us that a people and a nation are not identical. The English word "nation" can be used with the same meaning as the Japanese minzoku (people), and the English phrase "national character" can be translated into Japanese as kokumin-sei, used in almost the same way as *minzoku,* but in Japanese *kokumin* (nation) and *minzoku* (people) as defined here do not coincide.

Even in present times, we witness the tragedies of peoples divided north and south into two separate nations. The Polish people in their past history have time and again been divided by stronger powers into separate nations. In fact, there is a European joke about the Poles' strong sense of nationalism. A certain magazine offered a prize for an essay on the elephant. The German contributed a hundred-page monograph entitled "An Introduction to the Study of the Ecological Attributes of the Elephant." The Frenchman wrote a witty story about the love life of the elephant. But the Pole wrote on "The Elephant and the Problem of Polish National Self-Determination." Indeed, every topic became relevant to Polish national self-determination or the overriding desire for unification. In neighboring China, a well-known phrase is "The Harmony of Five Peoples," which expresses the ideal of a single nation embodying the harmony of the five great peoples: the Han, the peoples of Manchuria, Mongolia, Tibet, and the Uighur. The present Peking government has established an Institute for Ethnological Research and is educating students of ethnic minorities who are in the strict sense of the word non-Chinese.

Soviet Russia as a nation is also made up of many peoples, and the Union of Soviet Socialist Republics includes many self-governing bodies of different peoples. Thus, in this case too we cannot equate "nation" with "people." Yet, as in the previous case of a single people, the continuity of a shared communal life like that of the Japanese existing for a long period of time as a single political entity is also an important factor in the formation of a homogeneous people.

Further, if we turn to the case of the United States, I cannot help thinking that the national unification of the United States is a mighty force in the creation of a new people. Although we speak of "the American" today, we do not yet use the phrase "the American people." But are not the Americans today close to being a people, as we understand this concept? At the least, it seems probable that, in one or two centuries' time, they will be conscious of themselves as a single people.

At present, there is great racial diversity in America. A wide variety of different races and peoples have entered America from Europe and from Asia. The Negroes who are the descendants of black men brought to the New World as slaves now constitute a major problem. But in this melting pot of different races and different peoples, the same American English is spoken and the same American way of life is followed. It is possible to tell at a glance an American of European ancestry from a European: such are the changes that have come about in ways of thinking and feeling, in gestures, attitudes, and national character.

Will not these factors eventually serve to make a new people of the Americans? Were that to occur, I suspect we would agree that the national unification achieved by the United States would not be an irrelevant factor. However, as I said before, history teaches us that political unification does not necessarily lead to the formation of a single people.

Ethnic Solidarity through Religion or Language

Then, what other factors should we consider? Religion is one. It certainly appears that sharing the same religion is conducive to ethnic solidarity, as we see in the case of Judaism, which has very strong characteristics.

Whether in Babylonia or Egypt, or scattered to the corners of the world, the Jews have retained ethnic solidarity through their religion. However, in the case of the Japanese, the organic relationship between religion and people seems to be very tenuous. We have a traditional Shinto faith,[4] yet in our homes we place beside the Shinto altar[5] a Buddhist altar. We worship at both Shinto shrines and Buddhist temples. We ask a Shinto priest to offer a prayer at weddings but need the services of a Buddhist priest at funerals. This type of national characteristic seems to be rare, and it appears that the relationship between religious faith and ethnic consciousness is not very close in Japan.

If we take Christianity and Islam as examples, we find that the more they develop as world religions, the less religion and ethnic solidarity coincide. Consequently, even if we hold religion to be a causative factor, it is not easy to grasp what is basic to the formation of a people. Thus it becomes extremely difficult to define people.

However, the relevance of language as a factor has long been on my mind. There are certainly cases of one people, speaking a single language, later separating into two or more different peoples. The English and the Americans speak basically the same language but are now about to part ways for a variety of reasons. History points to many other such cases. But are there any cases, historical or contemporary, in which a people identified and classified as a single people is composed of more than two groups using different languages? I think it would be almost impossible to find such an example.

As a working hypothesis I would suggest that the use of a common language is one of the basic factors in the formation of a people. I have the impression that when a group loses its own distinctive language and begins to speak another language, it becomes a separate people. The Turkish Republic is a country with a strong national consciousness which achieved its independence after World War I, and its history goes back far beyond the Christian era. The Hittites, who figure in the Old Testament as the Heth, es-

4. The ancient native religion of Japan, modified later under the influence of Buddhism and Confucianism. "Shinto" means "the way of the gods," and its rituals and customs today include visits to shrines and the celebration of festivals. It is one of the basic elements of Japanese culture. The *Kojiki* (A.D. 712) and *Nihon-shoki* (A.D. 720) are the main literary sources for the nature mythology upon which the Shinto value system rests (for a more thorough description of these sources, see Chap. 2, n. 6). Its origins may go back to the early Christian centuries.

For the Japanese, Shinto is not so much a "private religion" as a "civil religion," as Robert Bellah points out. A Japanese Buddhist or Christian may look upon Shinto as an expression of his Japanese cultural heritage, "a religious dimension in the national sphere of life but one which does not exclude commitment to private and more universalistic religious positions." "Shinto could be presented as a national and civil approach to the transcendent which yet leaves the individual free to pursue his own individual quest for meaning and salvation" (Robert N. Bellah, "Shinto and Modernization," in *Proceedings: The Second International Conference for Shinto Studies, 1967* [Tokyo: Kokugakuin Daigaku Nihon Bunka Kenkyūsho, 1967], p. 161).

5. An altar enshrining the favorite gods of the family in a miniature Shinto shrine.

tablished a kingdom in Asia Minor, the heart of the present-day Turkish Republic, and were a great power which opposed the Egyptian pharaohs. Today the Turks acclaim the Hittite kingdom as being the golden age of their ancestors. Judged by the standards of modern scholarship, this is an illogicality, since the Hittite language was Indo-European, while Turkish belongs to the Altaic family of languages. Thus the two languages do not even belong to the same lineage. A wide chasm exists between the emergence of the Turkish people and the ancient Hittite kingdom.

When we turn to the Chinese, we discover that the case is different. As far back as a thousand and several hundred years before Christ, in the Yin era, a language basically the same as modern Chinese was already spoken. Numerous examples of the original forms of present-day Chinese characters have been found on scapuli among the Yin ruins. As a people, too, the Chinese, with the largest population in the world—well over six hundred million—possess the longest continuous existence.

Two Newspaper Articles

I would like to refer at this point to several newspaper articles supporting my theory which appeared after I had written on the relation between language and a people. The following passages are from one of them, entitled "Aikoku-shin to bokoku-go" [Patriotism and the mother tongue], contributed to the *Asahi* (May 13, 1964) by Tsunatoshi Furuya, the president of the Brazilian Nomura Trading Corporation, an establishment in São Paulo:

In 1937, I migrated to Brazil after receiving a college diploma, and by now I am the father of nisei of Brazilian nationality. Nowadays I find myself thinking about the meaning of the term "the Japanese" which we use quite casually. "Japan" is indeed the name of the organized entity which is the state. Then does the term "the Japanese" denote those who are of Japanese nationality? There are a great many people of Japanese nationality who cannot appropriately be called "Japanese," while we know many foreigners who do not have Japanese nationality yet who truly love Japan and have been longtime residents of Japan. Also, as the father of nisei children, I find from actual experience that I cannot accept the view that one can identify the Japanese through facial features and hair color. My children have Japanese features, but cannot truthfully be called "Japanese." In effect, what I am trying to say is that nationality and race are not the determining factors in deciding who is Japanese. Then what other criterion do we have? I should like to suggest the continuity of culture. The core of a culture is language, so that, in other words, the Japanese language is the determining factor in characterizing the Japanese.

Everybody possesses one language that helps to mature him and this I call the "mother tongue" or the "first language"; it is distinct from the "second language" or a "foreign language." However fluent a man may be in several languages, he is bound to have a single "mother tongue." If someone were to claim to have two "mother tongues," I would say that he did not have even one "mother tongue." The mother tongue indeed comprises the sphere of culture which binds people together. I think the Japanese are those whose "mother tongue" is Japanese, and who belong to the Japanese cultural sphere.

Although some revisions need to be made in regard to certain words or phrases, Furuya's views are close to those I have explained. He continues:

> I think the "mother tongue" of a person is determined by the environment in which he lives from the age of about fifteen to the age at which he finishes his university education. This opinion may be slightly controversial, since some might judge that childhood is the more crucial period, but should anyone spend the period I first mentioned [namely, from age fifteen to twenty-two] in America, regardless of his physical features or his nationality, the "mother tongue" of this person would be American English and he would have matured within the matrix of American culture. I would call this person an American. Brazilian is the mother tongue of my own children. (Strictly speaking, Brazilian is very close to Portuguese, but the differences between the two languages approximate the differences between the Queen's English and American English. The same applies to Spanish. So we use the term "Brazilian.") My children are, therefore, Brazilian. If they are taught the Japanese language, it should be presented to them as a foreign language. In my own case, since I passed the crucial years in Japan, I cannot claim any language but Japanese as my "mother tongue." The Japanese language and Japanese culture matured me.

> Japanese who have spent several decades abroad and who have mature nisei children are Japanese themselves, but their children are not Japanese. This consciousness is shared by many issei in California and Hawaii, and it gives rise to many problems. It is not merely a problem of nationality. It is a problem deeper than nationality, a problem of culture, whose medium is language, and a problem of a people's character.

In the series called "Amerika tsūshin" [Letters from America] in the *Asahi* (May, June 1965), literary critic Jun Etō discusses the same problem in terms of his experience at Princeton:

> Through discipline and effort, I may be able to perfect my inadequate English. Even now, from sheer necessity, I think in English. But what Richard Blackmur calls "the silent language," that is, the abyss that exists before thought takes shape, is in my case ultimately Japanese. And when language is divorced from the "silence," it cannot, strictly speaking, function as literature. The reason for this is that, through this silent segment, I am in touch with the cultural accumulation that the Japanese language has amassed.

These views expressed by Etō coincide with my own ideas and writings.

Language as a Basic Factor in the Formation of a People

We may thus say that a common language is an extremely basic, perhaps even a determining, factor, granted that it is not the only factor, in the evolution of a people as a single cultural community. At the same time, this approach is related to the very large scholarly issue of language and culture, or the role of language in a particular culture. In fact, the relationship between language and culture has recently been the subject of close anthropological study, which is likely to be very suggestive for the field of Japanese folklore.

Yanagita started a long time ago to compile a vast dictionary of Japanese phrases related to Japanese folkways. It is an extensive collection covering dialectal variants that we cannot find in ordinary dictionaries. I suspect that the question of the living use of this dictionary within the framework of Japanese culture and its use as a tool in the analysis of Japanese culture will become themes for future research in the field of Japanese folklore.

It is a formidable task to deal with the grammatical structure of the Japanese language and the Japanese vocabulary in relation to the individual characteristics of Japanese culture. However, I feel it is time for the appearance of ambitious scholars ready to tackle this problem with enthusiasm. Given the appropriate conditions, I would like to pursue research of this kind myself.

To return to the problem of who the Japanese are, or how we can define the Japanese people, I think we may conclude that the Japanese are those people whose mother tongue is Japanese, who grew up within its context, and who assimilated Japanese culture through the medium of the Japanese language. A precondition for the emergence of such Japanese is that they pursue a communal life in the same region for some length of time. It is not possible for a people to be formed of peoples living in far distant places from the beginning.

The phrase "the same region" does not necessarily mean living face to face within the same village, but it is necessary for people to be close enough to share the same culture, both directly and indirectly: the same way of life, a common language, and a common history and tradition. In other words, there should be a group that shares a common destiny.

Unification into a single state and racial identity are conditions that would help to strengthen the bonds of a people. It would be more difficult for white and black races to build a nation than for races with similar physical features. However, knowledge of many peoples confirms the impression that racial homogeneity does not constitute the ultimate factor. A people can be formed without regard to nationality or race. This is where culture becomes a large issue, though, of course, within any culture a common language is a particularly important factor, not merely manners and customs in the widest sense.

Thus, we can classify peoples objectively according to the above criterion, but we find that, usually, the more powerful a people becomes, the more highly developed are the following subjective factors: a common feeling of belonging to a group, and a kindred consciousness, which might be termed "we feeling"—the feeling that "We are Japanese," or "We are the German people." This does not arise from factors such as race, nationality, or belief in a common religion alone. It is through such considerations that we may answer the question "Who are the Japanese?"

Of course, when men from Kagoshima Prefecture (Kyūshū) or Aomori Prefecture (northeastern Honshū) talk in pure dialect, the question of communication may arise, even among Japanese, but any group that we differentiate as a people necessarily possesses a common language. Dialects exist everywhere. In New York, a Southern dialect is often more difficult to understand than the English spoken by a Japanese.

Yet how can we draw the boundaries for the Japanese language? Surely they should delineate the sphere in which it can function, surmounting dialectal differences, as a possible standard language for communication. In Chinese, there is a gap in communication between north and south which is beyond anything we see in Japanese, yet there is a common grammatical structure, and the printed characters are the same everywhere. Though there are extreme differences between the dialects in pronunciation and other aspects, in general, Mandarin, the official Peking dialect, is the standard language in which men from Canton and Peking can converse freely. In addition, they read the same Chinese publications. This is what we mean by a people. We can assume the existence of a single language within a sphere where a common language functions transcending dialects. I do not believe there are any exceptions to this.

Having considered the question of defining the Japanese people spatially, as it were, we shall now trace back in time the problem of when the Japanese, according to our definition, actually became an identifiable people. In so doing, we immediately run up against the problem of the origins of this people. According to my definition of "people," this does not necessarily coincide with the origins of the Japanese nation, and the relation between the people and the nation is a separate question. I would now like to consider, starting with the problem of the origins of the Japanese people, the basic character of the Japanese through their two-thousand-year history, that is, their ethnic character—which will be the "pattern" of Japanese culture. This study will also cover the distinctive characteristics of the Japanese in contrast to those of the neighboring peoples of Asia, or to those of the peoples of Europe, which have loomed so large in the Japanese consciousness since the Meiji era.

2. The Formation of the Japanese People

The Settlement of the "Japanese"

I will not be dealing with the formation of the Japanese people, that is, the origins of the Japanese, in the sense of the origins of man in the Japanese islands. I intend rather to look into the problem of when we can first discover evidence of a people distinctly recognizable as Japanese, or as the Japanese people, and to trace the formation of this people. Of course, it may not be possible to make a complete scholarly explanation based on presently available information, but I would like to see how far we can proceed by synthesizing all the knowledge available to us.

Obviously, the confines of a single scholarly discipline are quite inadequate for the solution of this problem. For instance, reliance upon the study of Japanese folklore alone or comparative ethnology by itself will not be adequate. A synthesis of the knowledge obtained through archaeology, history, and other disciplines is necessary; and beyond these disciplines, subsuming and synthesizing them, should be a field such as cultural history. My knowledge of Japanese folklore is not great, nor is my knowledge of archaeology and history. My specialization, if I might call it so, is in the field of cultural anthropology, and though I spent rather a long time studying ethnology previously, I would hesitate to call this my special discipline. I have thus

/c

accumulated a heterogeneous store of knowledge, while cherishing the dream of synthesizing the fruits of these various disciplines, but I have not yet been able to dig deeply into any one discipline. Nonetheless, I feel that a methodology based on this synthetic approach would be very valuable in building the structure of cultural history.

To return to the problem of the formation and origins of the Japanese people, it is often said that until World War II research into the origins of the Japanese was taboo. As I have written elsewhere, this is not strictly true. I myself in my first year at primary school was taught the origins of the Japanese people. Then again I learned in my Japanese history lessons in the fifth and sixth grades about the beginnings of Japan, the formation of the people and the nation; that is, how the goddess Amaterasu,[1] who lived in the High Heavenly Plains, sent her grandson, Ninigi-no-mikoto, to earth with a declaration that the Japanese islands were a fit habitation for her descendants. This was the famous descent upon Mount Takachiho of Hiuga (in Kyūshū), and her descendants, in obeisance to her declaration, achieved the unification of the country. Morever, we learned that Prince Hatsu-kuni-shirasu-sumera, the first emperor of Japan (later called Emperor Jimmu), had left Hiuga and conquered western Japan, passing through the Inland Sea and establishing his capital in Yamato.[2] The unification of the land was achieved through the cession of land to the new reigning powers—the heavenly descendants from the High Heavenly Plains—by the previously established local tribal chiefs, the kunitsukami, represented by Ōkuni-nushi of Izumo.[3] Such is the legend of land cession, and after these events the emperors sent out generals who gradually subdued and unified Japan.

This is what we were taught about the formation and origins of the Japanese people and their nation,

1. The Sun Goddess, from whom, according to the mythology narrated in the chronicles of the Kojiki and the Nihonshoki, the emperors of Japan are descended.

2. The area south of Kyoto around Nara, one of the ancient capitals of Japan, is known as the Yamato Plain. According to Japanese tradition, Yamato was the site of the final settlement of the conquering tribal group which came from Kyūshū along the Inland Sea to its eastern end. The Yamato rulers are the ancestors of the imperial family, and Yamato later became a synonym for Japan.

3. Ōkuni-nushi was the son of Susano-o, the brother of the Sun Goddess, Amaterasu; he ruled over Izumo on the western shores of Honshū, the main island of Japan. The legends about Ōkuni-nushi suggest an important local power who surrendered to the Yamato rulers, though peaceably and not through military conquest (for a more thorough discussion, see Chap. 4, nn. 23 and 24). The study of the Korean affiliations of Ōkuni-nushi and his descendants has only just begun. The legends record traffic between Izumo and Korea which reflects early contacts and continental influence upon Japan.

and there was certainly no taboo on discussion of the origins and formation of the Japanese.

In the postwar period, however, education has changed completely, and these legends are now regarded as the pseudo-history of the Japanese ruling class, with no scientific value. The postwar generation has been taught about the Jōmon Age, succeeded by the Yayoi Age. The historical chronology is as follows: the Jōmon Age, the Yayoi Age, the Tomb Age, followed by the Nara and Heian periods.[4]

Not long ago, an archaeological discovery revealed the existence of a pre-Jōmon age, that is, the remains of human beings in Japan belonging to an age preceding the Jōmon Culture Age. The existence of a pre-pottery culture was confirmed, starting with discoveries at Iwajuku in Gumma Prefecture, and subsequently supported by other discoveries ranging from Hokkaidō in the north to Kyūshū in the south, and even in Korea. Thus, Japanese history textbooks now begin with pre-Jōmon culture. This is the scientific explanation of the origins of the Japanese people.

However, even in prewar Japan this kind of archaeological research was not actually suppressed. There are, for instance, the remarkable documentary studies of Sōkichi Tsuda[5] entitled *Jindai-shi no kenkyū* [A new study of the theocratic period] and *Kiki no kenkyū* [A new study of the *Kojiki* and the *Nihon-shoki*]. His publications were censored and the professor himself was brought to trial on the grounds that his works violated the "spirit of clarification of the national polity."[6] Thus, the study of mythology was suppressed, but scholarly reports on archaeological findings continued to be published.

4. For a description and chronology of these periods, see Appendix A.

5. 1873–1961. Tsuda was a professor at Waseda University whose penetrating analyses and interpretations of Japanese and Chinese classics expressed a critical attitude that was not welcomed by the contemporary governmental authorities. His works were banned and he was later expelled from the university.

Tsuda's studies were based on the findings of many other scholars and were supported by detailed evidence. Since his works were addressed to other scholars, for some time after their publication they attracted no attention outside academic circles. Yet he had subjected to scrutiny the absolute authority of the emperor established by the Meiji Constitution. When militarists and rightists became active in the 1930s, they criticized Tsuda's works as an infringement of the sanctity of the imperial family. Tsuda and his publisher, Shigeo Iwanami, were brought to trial in 1940.

6. Tsuda's research on the sources of the *Kojiki* and the *Nihon-shoki* led him to question their historical validity at certain points. The *Kojiki*, or "Records of Ancient Matters," completed in A.D. 712, was based on Shinto traditions orally transmitted for centuries and on earlier historical sources, including the *Teiki* (imperial genealogies) and the *Kyūji* (ancient tales). Later, the compilation of another, more extensive history was undertaken. The result was the *Nihon-shoki* (or *Nihongi*), "Chronicles of Japan," which drew on Korean and Chinese sources as well as on those common to the *Kojiki*. According to Tsuda, sections of one of the sources for these two histories, the *Kyūji*, especially those passages dealing with mythology, ap-

The Interpretations in Postwar Textbooks

In the textbooks and surveys of so-called scientific postwar Japanese history, it has been accepted that the men who first left signs of their existence in the Japanese islands were Japanese. The way of life of these human beings, it is said, was evolved solely within the Japanese islands, as they built up a society with a stratified class structure in the course of expanding their productivity. Eventually, in the Tomb Age, the imperial family established itself as a ruling class over Japan. In other words, from the distant ages of pre-Jōmon culture, the ancestors of the present Japanese have gradually developed their ways of living within the Japanese islands and, with the extension of their sphere of activity, have formed a nation. This is the supposedly scientific interpretation found in the majority of postwar textbooks.

Yet when we speak of the pre-Jōmon age, we may note that Chōsuke Serizawa[7] recently discovered at Hayamizudai in Oita Prefecture paleolithic tools which, from the viewpoint of antiquity, are nothing like the previous discoveries of the pre-Jōmon age. They are so old that they belong to the earliest period of the early paleolithic age in world history, actually hundreds of thousands of years ago. In fact, the forms of these stone implements are as primitive as those discovered at Chouk'ou-tien near Peking, belonging to *Sinanthropus pekinensis,* and even though fossilized human remains have not yet been discovered, there has been further confirmation of the hypothesis that the distant ancestors of man lived in the Japanese islands in that age. Thus, according to these units of time, the ancestors of the Japanese were not merely the men of the Jōmon Age but men who can be traced back to *Sinanthropus* or *Pithecanthropus,* hundreds of thousands of years ago, or even to a more distant age.

peared to have been fabricated by the sixth-century imperial court for the purpose of showing that the emperors had ruled the land since the timeless past.

7. 1919—. Professor of Tōhoku University. An archaeologist who has written on the Stone Age in Japan and on pre-pottery culture.

However, mankind had not then reached the stage of being classified as *Homo sapiens,* that is, the same species as modern man; mankind was at an earlier stage in the evolution to *Homo sapiens,* though scholars differ in their estimates as to which stage this was. In any case, men using stone implements lived hundreds of thousands of years ago in the Japanese islands. The question is, Were these men the ancestors of the Japanese people?

If we trace our ancestry back far enough, we will certainly find that we evolved from a higher species of animals who lived in the treetops. Of this there is no doubt; I am not trying to argue this point. Suppose, however, that a teacher in a high school tried to teach the beginnings of Japanese history in the pre-Jōmon period or in the Jōmon Age according to the above-mentioned kind of textbook or survey. If I were his pupil, I might ask, "Did the people of the Jōmon Age speak Japanese?" This is a question that no scholar can answer. Thus, if the teacher replied that he did not know, that would be an honest answer; but if he replied, "Of course they spoke Japanese," I, the pupil, might respond, "But what evidence is there that the people of the Jōmon Age spoke Japanese?" If the teacher lost his temper at this point, there would be nothing more to say. However, a conscientious teacher would probably answer, "Well, I don't believe we have any evidence. I must think about that question." This would indeed be the proper attitude for a teacher to take.

I myself hold no brief for dogmatic assertions of scholarship maintaining that the Jōmon Age people were the direct ancestors of the present Japanese, and on reading books by scholars writing coolly in this vein, I feel inclined to tease them with questions such as those above. So-called progressive archaeologists hold that a matrilineal tribal system existed in the Jōmon Age, and that, with the development of agriculture in the Yayoi Age and increasing division of labor and class conflicts, society then shifted to a patrilineal system, the family system evolving within a clan society. Yet there is no certain proof among the archaeological remains of pottery and stone implements or dwelling sites of whether the people living there determined kinship through the mother's line. After weighing these questions, what significance and limits would present-day anthropology attach to terms like "the age of clan society," and what relation would this age have to archaeological periodization? Whenever I read the unquestioned assumptions of Japanese history books narrating without any evidence the autogenic transition of the Jōmon culture to the Yayoi culture, and continuing to mark the stages of evolution from the Tomb Age into the historic period, I feel strongly skeptical. In fact, I have often raised questions like these, but no scholar has yet brought forward any counterarguments based on scholarly evidence.

My Own Views on the Origins of the Japanese

Before presenting my own views on the origins of the Japanese, I should perhaps make it clear that there are two separate problems: first, how the Japanese people were formed in the sense that I have already described, and, second, when human beings first came to inhabit the Japanese islands and to which race they belonged. The latter is a question of the origins of mankind, not the origins of the Japanese.

From this viewpoint, it becomes extremely doubtful whether the archaeological periodization of the pre-Jōmon, Jōmon, Yayoi, and Tomb Ages can be adopted as marking stages in a unilineal evolution of culture entirely within the Japanese islands, from a timeless past.

Of course, this kind of evolution is possible in the history of mankind. Yet, within a larger perspective, viewing Japan in the context of the cultural history of the Eurasian continent, the Japanese archipelago constitutes a blind alley for the civilization of Eurasia, and countless times in the past and in recent history waves of various new cultures arising on the continent have washed the shores of the Japanese islands. Since only the Pacific Ocean lies to the east of the archipelago, these cultures have been unable to spread beyond the islands and have thus accumulated here to help form the Japanese culture of today. This is true of both the historic and the modern periods, and evidence from the prehistoric era also corroborates this.

Should we then cling to the interpretation that from the beginning a people called the Japanese lived in Japan, and that foreign culture crossed the sea like mailed packages to be received and opened by these people? In my own view, and that of many anthropologists, one simply cannot understand the successive appearance of aspects of continental cultures in Japan sometime after their rise elsewhere unless one assumes that human beings crossed the seas bearing their culture.

The process of assimilation of Western culture after the Meiji era is well known. It is also a historical fact that between the Nara and Meiji periods there were no large immigrations of alien people through enemy infiltration or conquest. If we consider the prehistoric Yayoi period and the still earlier Jōmon period, however, it becomes extremely difficult to obtain any certain evidence about such factors; and if we consult archaeological materials, again and again problems arise that cannot be understood without assuming the transmigration of men bearing new cultures. According to carbon-14 dating, the beginnings of the Jōmon period date back ten thousand years, and the history of Japanese ceramics appears to be far longer than was indicated by the previous estimates of Japanese archaeologists. Further, returning to the central problem of this chapter, the changes and developments that mark the transition from the Jōmon to the Yayoi period, the explanation given by the majority of surveys and textbooks, that the Jōmon people either accepted new agricultural techniques—especially the techniques of irrigated rice cultivation—or invented these techniques themselves, is not completely satisfactory. I cannot assume that these Jōmon people developed a new agrarian culture entirely on their own.

As I mentioned before, I think the viewpoint of most anthropologists is that Japan's cultural history should be examined in close relation to the cultural history of the Eurasian continent, with the following questions in mind. What kind of cultural waves entered Japan from the continent, and when? By what peoples were they transmitted and by what route did they come? On the other hand, the approaches taken by so-called historical ethnology are hardly acceptable. It tries to achieve the reconstruction of ancient cultural history solely through ethnological classification of the cultural strata of Japan, contrasting the variety of customs and traditions found in present-day Japan with those of neighboring peoples—such as those revealed in ethnological data on Melanesia or various regions of Southeast Asia—which lead to the conclusion that certain cultural elements or combinations of elements entered Japan in the Jōmon period and survive today, and that such-and-such cultural constituents entered before that period. It would indeed be very interesting if these approaches were viable from the standpoint of scholarship, and I used to study with this in mind, but I have by now completely lost confidence in this kind of methodology, which lacks academic validity, and I shall not pursue it in the future. Consequently, we are left in the position of giving priority to archaeological clues and, for more recent ages, available documentary materials. This means leaving certain unsolved problems of the past unsolved, which appears at present to be the most appropriate scholarly attitude available.

When Did the Japanese People Appear?

I am afraid my introduction has become rather long, so let us now return to the central question: When indeed did the Japanese people appear as a recognizable racial group? From historic times, for instance the Nara period, documents survive, and no one will doubt that the language of that age is continuous with the modern Japanese language or that the people of that time were the ancestors of the present Japanese. But if we go back further to see how long ago we can ascertain the existence of a people recognizable as Japanese according to our definition in the previous chapter, I think the Yayoi Culture Age of the archaeologists affords us a significant clue. In fact, I think we can conclude that the people whose legacy is the culture of that age, whose village life was based on irrigated rice cultivation, were the ancestors of the present Japanese. There is enough scholarly evidence for this.

Consequently, the problem of the formation of the Japanese people becomes the problem of the formation of the Yayoi culture. How did this Yayoi Age begin, and how did the people of this age spread through the Japanese islands? When these questions are solved, then we can investigate the Yayoi Age in relation to the culture and people of the Jōmon Age, which preceded it.

The Yayoi Age lasted for at least five centuries, from about 200 B.C. to about A.D. 300. Concerning this period there are two great facts of which we can be certain. The first is the existence of the cultivation of rice, which is also a central problem in the discipline of Japanese folklore. With rice cultivation, almost all the basic techniques that have supported agricultural life until the most recent age of electricity were perfected in the Yayoi Age. Second is the problem of language already mentioned. We may consider the language spoken by the people of the Yayoi Age to be the same language that has been in use continuously from the Nara period to the present day.

On the basis of the above two facts, I believe we may safely say that a people recognizable as the same race as the present-day Japanese were living in the Japanese islands during the Yayoi Age.

Let us consider first the features of a society whose life is based upon wet rice production. Scorched grains of rice and husks of rice, or carbonized grains, have been discovered in the dwelling sites of this period. Also, traces of rice husks have been discovered on the bottoms of many Yayoi pots. I imagine that these impressions were made when pots were placed upon the rice husks before the clay hardened. Furthermore, new agricultural tools which did not exist in the Jōmon period have been found in Yayoi sites. Stone axes which can be used as agricultural hoes or sickles, and a half-moon-shaped stone knife which is called a cutter and is used to clip off the ears of grain appeared in this age. On the evidence of such excavated implements, we can surmise that grain was cultivated in this period.

In addition, Yayoi pottery has very different characteristics from Jōmon period pottery. There are, for example, pots with shapes suitable for steaming grain. These are pots perforated at the bottom which can be placed on top of pots with solid bottoms in which hot water can be boiled. This is evidence that grain was cooked.

Then again, discoveries have been made of group settlements like the site at Toro in Shizuoka Prefecture, where there is clear evidence of paddy-field rice cultivation. The remains of a rather large rice field with paths reinforced by rows of stakes have been discovered. Further, in the summer of 1965, an irrigation ditch was discovered. This evidence leads us to the conclusion that rice cultivation was undoubtedly practiced in the Yayoi period.

What I would like to emphasize, however, is not the single cultural fact of rice cultivation but the basic skills of the people who conducted such cultivation. Rice production no doubt formed the basis of the skills essential to daily life in the Yayoi Age, but Yayoi culture itself cannot be equated with rice cultivation. More important is the kind of system of daily living which was formed with rice cultivation at its center.

The Basic Skills of the Yayoi Period: The Economy

We may now draw certain conclusions based on the specific characteristics of the remains of the Yayoi Age. There was occupational specialization among, for example, potters, woodworkers, and blacksmiths, who made the tools of iron, copper, and bronze that replaced the stone implements like the stone cutter and stone ax mentioned before.

A clay spindle-whorl has also been found; a thin rod passes through a hole in the middle of a round or cone-shaped weight, which twists it like a top. The cottonlike fiber attached to the rod is twisted into thread by the spinning motion, working on the same general principle as the spindles used in present-day spinning factories. Clay spindle whorls attached to the rodlike parts, belonging to a certain period of the Yayoi Age, have also been excavated in large numbers.

This method of spinning can be found in various regions of the world even today and is much used in western Asia. On our research expeditions in Latin America, in the rural districts of the Andes and of Mexico, we often saw women sitting outside their houses talking and spinning. Afterward they wove the thread on handmade looms. Such spinning skills are found wherever weaving is practiced, and in Japan the spinning whorl first appeared in the Yayoi Age.

Further, there is evidence of weaving as well. Hand-woven cloth of fine texture has survived, preserved under special conditions; and there are potsherds that reveal the fine mesh-lines of cloth, which were probably made by covering baskets with cloth and molding clay within these forms to shape pots. During the Meiji era, housewives used to weave their families' clothing on handmade looms. By now, the use of clothing manufactured by textile factories has become universal in Japan, and these domestic scenes have vanished, but such skills as spinning and weaving had already made their appearance in the villages of the Yayoi Age.

What kind of houses did the people of the Yayoi Age live in? The sites of pit dwellings and caves have been excavated, but the original shape of the houses cannot be restored with only the relics of pillars to guide us. There are models of restored houses in museums, but I do not know how accurate they are. Nonetheless, I think the pattern of daily life of this age which can be reconstructed from the archaeological remains basically differs little from the life of the Japanese rice-growing farmers of the historic period up to modern times. Of course, we may assume that there were fishing villages as well, and that other plants besides rice were cultivated.

In Japanese villages traditional rice rituals and annual ceremonies are performed in connection with the stages of rice cultivation from planting to harvesting. However, it is not possible to trace a direct relationship between the artifacts discussed above and the traditional world view and mental attitudes of the rural folk which underlie these practices. We still do not know exactly when these customs originated in Japan.

Some of the customs followed in Japanese villages closely resemble those of the various peoples in the rice-growing regions stretching from Okinawa throughout south and southwest China; there is, in particular, a marked resemblance to the practices found in Southeast Asia and Indonesia, where wet rice cultivation is practiced. Can we build any hypothesis, based on these facts, about the origins of these customs in Japan? Although we lack documentary or archaeological evidence, we can at least surmise that the traditional mental outlook of the Japanese began to develop in the Yayoi Age where we find clear evidence of rice cultivation, that is, from about the beginning of the Christian era.

I have my doubts about the use of comparative ethnological materials to analyze the distant past, but the probabilities of fruitful research are comparatively great if the past reaches only as far back as the Yayoi Age. Should our understanding of cultural structures lead to the discovery of universal principles, then the mental outlook of the Yayoi people may become clearer. It would not be illogical to hypothesize that, if certain basic factors in rice-growing villages constitute a culture complex, then there would exist a corresponding mental outlook and religion. These are the special characteristics of the Yayoi Age which constitute clues to the existence of the Japanese as we know them today, based on the above-mentioned aspects of skills and the economy.

The Japanese Language in the Yayoi Age

4 >

4/7

The other great problem is that of the Japanese language. I would like to explain why I think that the Japanese language was spoken in the Yayoi Age. Evidence supporting my hypothesis is scarce compared with that in the fields of technology and economy. But records of the life of the western Japanese in Kyūshū exist in a Chinese chronicle dating from the third century, that is, the late Yayoi Age. This chronicle is the *Wajin-den* of the *Tōi-den* of the *Gishi*.[8] There are several words in the *Wajin-den* that can be interpreted as attempts to record the pronunciation of the Japanese language of that time. These form the basis for scholars' hypotheses that the language of the Yayoi Age is continuous with the Japanese language of today.

However, there have been various theories as to the credibility of the *Wajin-den*. Some suspect that information about lands other than Japan might have been mixed into it; but there is persuasive evidence counterbalancing these doubts. The names of places, from the south of Korea to the islands of Tsushima and Iki in the Tsushima Straits, as well as Matsuura in Kyūshū, correspond to later Japanese place names. It is also recorded that there were about thirty small local units like the Wajin countries which extended under various names from Tsushima and Iki to the west of Japan. The official names of these countries are written in Chinese characters, and sometimes names of people also appear. In these official names are constituents that correspond to later Japanese nouns and adjectives, and the typical Japanese word order, in which the noun follows the adjective, is quite clear. Several words appear which support these points. For instance, we find the word *hiko,* which in Old Japanese signifies man, in contradistinction to *hime* [Old Japanese for woman]; also, the word *hinamori* was used to describe the rank of an official. These

8. The *Wajin-den* [On the people of Wa] is a section of the *Tōi-den* [On the Eastern Barbarians], which, in turn, is a chapter of the *Wei chih* [Records of Wei] (in Japanese, *Gishi*). The *Gishi* is itself a part of the Chinese historical work *San-kuo chih* [History of the Three Kingdoms], compiled at the close of the third century. The author, Ch'en Shou 233–297), describes the Japanese islands and people, and the relations of the Wei state with the land of Wa (i.e., Japan), called Yamatai-koku. The *Wajin-den* is valuable as one of the rare, and extended, descriptions of the Japanese in the early centuries of the Christian era, when the Japanese themselves were still nonliterate.

must be attempts to express the pronunciation of
the Japanese in Chinese characters, an interpretation that is supported by many scholars. In addition, though there is some uncertainty about the
significance of this, such words as *nakatomi, shimako,
hitoko, tama,* and *mininari* appear. These are recorded as the names of ranks of officials in Wa.
Therefore, they are not Chinese but Chinese
renderings of the Wa people's language. Furthermore, among these words are several whose
continuity with the Japanese language of the post-
Nara period can be traced. This is only scanty
evidence, but it is all we have. Also, the terms
Yamatai-koku[9] and *himiko* are neither Chinese nor
Korean. Surely we may interpret these as Japanese.
And should this interpretation be correct, it would
indicate that the meaning of the words and even
the structural word order of this time show continuity with the Japanese language of the post-Nara
period. This evidence leads to the conclusion that
the Japanese of the Yayoi Age, at least the Wajin
of western Japan, spoke the Japanese language as
we know it today.

We may conclude, then, that the Japanese of the
Yayoi Age practiced an agriculture based on rice
cultivation which differed little from that of the
Japanese of the historic period, and that they spoke
Japanese. We may accept these as facts. I find,
however, that I cannot go beyond this to the
acceptance of theories about the beginnings of the
family in this age, or about the kinship structure and
whether it was matrilineal or patrilineal. I feel like
inquiring what evidence can be brought forward
to support such theories.

9. Meaning, "the land of Wa."
Some scholars identify Yamatai-
koku with part of Kyūshū and
others with Yamato. For centuries, scholars have debated this,
since the directions and distances
given in the *Wei chih's* descriptions of the location of Yamatai
can be interpreted to apply to
either Kyūshū or Yamato. The
description of local customs in
Yamatai, in any case, gives a
picture of early Japanese society
which is based on the reports of
officials or traders who had
traveled to Japan. The information is similar to what is
known of early Japanese life from
literary sources and shows the
remarkable continuity of Japanese
culture. Yamatai may be considered an archetype of Japanese
culture.

The Records of the *Wajin-den*

4c

If we study the *Wajin-den*, we find various clues as to the climate and soil of the country of Wa and the life of the people of Wa. The Iwanami Bunko edition of the *Wajin-den* prints both the original Chinese and the Japanese translation, with notes on a few words and phrases, some of which serve to illustrate aspects of this study and offer interesting insights.

For instance, it is recorded that the land of Wa is very warm and that the people eat raw vegetables both in winter and in summer. This would not apply to northern Japan, but it is an observation applicable to western Japan and lands farther south. Again, it is recorded that the people of Wa liked to dive into the deeper waters and catch fish and abalone. These activities are similar to those of the divers in various parts of Japan today. About villages, the record tells us that rice and flax were planted. Silkworms were raised and silk was made from the fiber spun; fine linen thread and cotton were also spun. Thus, it appears that most of our main activities of the historic period already existed at this time.

However, in regard to animals, the record explains that there were no cattle, horses, tigers, leopards, sheep, or magpies in that land, and indeed we can confirm that there were no tigers or leopards in the Japanese islands. As for sheep, we can see from the number of entries pertaining to sheep in a Chinese dictionary what an important base of economic life they constituted on the Chinese continent. In Japan, however, it was probably only after the beginning of the Meiji era that sheep began to be kept. Some skeletons of cattle and horses have been excavated, but the archaeological remains suggest that in early Japanese agricultural life there was little reliance upon livestock. Despite the constant warfare of this age, cavalry appears not to have existed. This lack of cattle and horses is significant in relation to agriculture and livestock and forms the basic motif of my study of Japanese culture.

Next, let us consider the customs of the people. There is a method of divination by tortoiseshell called *ki-boku*, which survives even today in Japanese shrines. Bones are burned, good or bad fortunes foretold, and the results reported to the gods. Then the cracks in the bones resulting from the burning are used for divining auguries. This is the same as the practice of bone oracles performed in China in the Yin period,[10] where the shoulder bones of cattle and sheep or the tortoiseshell seem to have been used. In this oracular method, first the letters called shell-bone script, which are the original forms of the Chinese characters, were written on the bones or tortoiseshell; when these were placed over a fire, the heat caused cracks to form. The oracles pertaining to such great issues of state as the rights and wrongs of conducting wars, politics, and the travel of kings were gleaned through reading the relation between the cracks and the letters. We do not know whether this custom originated in China or not, but it is widespread among the peoples of northern Asia.

In addition, ethnologists inform us that there is a custom called "scapulimancy," in which good and bad are foretold through bone oracles of deer and other animals, practiced at present from Siberia to North America. The "scapula" is a shoulder bone, and this mode of bone oracle is called "scapuling." A study on the extent of this custom was published long ago by Robert H. Lowie.[11]

In Japan, this custom appears to have been practiced in ancient times. It is described, for instance, in the *Kojiki*. When the goddess Amaterasu concealed herself in a cave, the eight hundred myriad gods assembled at the Ame-no-yasu-no-kawara [dry bed of the river Ame-no-yasu; the

10. The Yin (also known as Shang) dynasty of China ruled from c. 1766 to c. 1122 B.C., or, according to some modern scholars, from c. 1523 to c. 1027 B.C.

11. 1883–1957. As professor of anthropology at the University of California in Berkeley, 1921–50, he contributed to the development of cultural anthropology.

words "Ame-no" indicate a connection with the heavenly abode of the gods] and held a conference. The passage that follows can be interpreted as a description of the performance of this bone oracle, the gods taking counsel on how to lead the Sun Goddess, Amaterasu, out of the cave:

> Then, the two deities Amenokoyane-no-mikoto and Futotama-no-mikoto conducted divination by burning a complete shoulder bone of a stag of Mount Ame-no-kagu in the fire of ame-no-hahaka taken from Mount Ame-no-kagu. And according to the telling, a thick sacred tree was uprooted at Mount Ame-no-kagu.[12]

The "ame-no-hahaka" of Mount Ame-no-kagu is written with the characters for scarlet cherry blossom, so one can interpret this passage as describing an oracle performed by laying the shoulder bone of a deer upon a fire made by burning a cherry tree. Knowledge of the method of Chinese oracles has been handed down in Japanese shrines, and the custom of bone oracles is widespread among the neighboring peoples of Japan to the north. This evidence that the Wa people of southwestern Japan already practiced divining by bone oracles is a very interesting fact of cultural history.

The customs of the Wa people described in the *Wajin-den* almost all show continuity with those of South and Southeast Asia, but only this scapulimancy can be tied to northern Asia as well. This custom, together with the metal implements of the Yayoi Age, must be evidence of the influence of China in early Japan. The record of the *Wajin-den* seems to be of rather high credibility.

In addition, we may note from our knowledge of ethnology that many customs of south China, Southeast Asia, and the western Pacific area are described in the *Wajin-den* as customs of the people

12. *Kojiki*, translated and annotated by Shunji Inoue (rev. ed.; Fukuoka: Nihon Shūji Kyōiku Renmei, 1966), p. 39.

of Wa. For instance, all males, both adults and children, tattooed their faces and bodies. This custom of tattooing appears to have been very strange to the Chinese. In the land of the Southern Barbarians south of the Yangtze River, the custom of tattooing was accepted, so that in the Analects[13] and in Mencius[14] the tattooing practiced by the Wa people of Japan was regarded as a "barbaric" custom.

There is a close relation between this custom of tattooing and the Wa divers I mentioned before as being described in the *Wajin-den*. According to the *Wajin-den*, the divers tattooed themselves in order to escape the big fish and sea birds when they dived for fish, abalone, and clams. Thus, it was first done to ward off the attacks of large fish like sharks, or large birds, and for magical purposes, and later it became purely decorative.

As for the dress of the people of Wa, the men merely covered their heads with cotton cloth and tied a wide band of unsewn cloth round their bodies. The description of the garment is not clear. The women's hair was either loose or tied in a knot, and for their dress they simply put their heads through a slit made in the middle of a length of cloth. This is still a widespread custom throughout the world. Even today the descendants of the Inca in South America make a cloak of this kind called a "poncho," which they put on over the head. It is made of cloth dyed with gay patterns and woven from the wool of llama or alpaca, members of the camel family. This type of dress is spread through Southeast Asia and was used in Japan also; material evidence as well as the *Wajin-den* confirm this.

Thus, it is possible to interpret the *Wajin-den* in many ways. Some scholars have claimed that its descriptions refer not only to Japan but also to the customs of south China and Southeast Asia. Other well-known theories state that the Chinese thought

13. A collection of sayings attributed to Confucius (c. 551–479 B.C.).

14. 371–288? B.C. A Chinese sage whose writings are contained in *The Book of Mencius*.

of the people of Wa as not only inhabiting Kyūshū, Japan, but also spreading far to the south, or that the accounts of customs of peoples other than the Wa are inaccurate.

Also, in regard to the position of the kingdom of Wa, some have suggested that it was near the present Hainan Island in the South China Sea. It has also been contended that "calculation of the distance shows the position [of Wa] to be east of Hoichi." Hoichi Tongyhe is south of the lower reaches of the Yangtze River, so this means that the land of Wa was located east of the lower reaches of the Yangtze River. This interpretation is not so far-fetched. The latitude of the southern part of Kyūshū is about the same as that of the mouth of the Yangtze River. It can be assumed that the Chinese thought of the land of Wa as being far east of the lower reaches of the Yangtze River. And the customs of the people of Wa are characteristically southern, as mentioned before.

If this record of the Wa people is a description of the people of western Kyūshū, we can assume that the life of western Japan at the end of the Yayoi Age had much in common with the life of the various agricultural peoples living in Southeast Asia today.

The *Giryaku* [*Wei-lüeh* in Chinese] is a historical work that survives only as a fragment in another book.[15] It relates that in the country of the Wa people, Kunakoku, "their ancient sayings state they are descendants of Taipo," and the phrase "ancient sayings" may mean "legends." This can be interpreted as the belief of the people in an ancestor, Taipo, the founder of Wu, a country south of the Yangtze River. This is merely a fragment, but it is of some significance when we consider the origins of the Japanese people.

Since there are further problems related to the formation of the Japanese people, the next chapter, "The Sources of Japanese Culture," will comple-

15. The *Wei-lüeh* recorded the history of Wei during the period of the Three Kingdoms (A.D. 220–280). It is said that the *San-kuo chih* [The history of the Three Kingdoms] was based upon this lost work.

ment this one in explaining my views on the
origins of the Japanese.

3. The Sources of Japanese Culture

The Broad Implications of Revolutions in Patterns of Living

I have assembled so far various materials drawn from the different fields of archaeology, history, folklore, and mythology and have explained the significance of the period during which a rice-based culture, designated Yayoi culture by archaeologists, spread in the Japanese islands. These materials form the bases for identifying the people later known as the Japanese with the people of Wa described in the Chinese chronicles. In other words, these are the grounds for the hypothesis that the Japanese people were formed in the Yayoi Age.

Did this cultural complex known as Yayoi culture, founded on the new irrigated rice production pattern of living, originate entirely within the Japanese islands independently of events in the outside world? If this were true, it would mean that the Jōmon people, living in the Japanese islands in the years before the Yayoi Age, had discovered how to raise rice within Japan and had invented the life skills that formed the foundation of later Japanese agriculture. Yet would this be likely, in view of our general knowledge of world history? Although many scholars may think this possible, this approach would be like a farfetched hypothesis that the Industrial Revolution in Russia, Japan, and other nations of the world developed independently of Western Europe. It would be like affirming that the Japanese—or the English or the Russians—had invented the steam engine through the development of their own distinctive culture. This, of course, is possible. However, a study of world history proves that the Industrial Revolution did not evolve through this kind of process. Since this happened only two or three hundred years ago, we know from documents and general knowledge handed down to us that the Industrial Revolution started in England and eventually spread throughout the world.

The development of agricultural skills related to the cultivation of grains was a major revolution in patterns of living that took place before the Industrial Revolution. In describing this, anthropologists use the phrase "agricultural revolution" in contrast to "industrial revolution," or "food production revolution" in contrast to a "food-collecting" economy. The development of grain-raising skills was a great turning point in the history of mankind in the period before the Industrial Revolution. If we search for another, earlier stage equal in significance to the agricultural revolution, it would be the time, several hundreds of thousands of years ago, when man, evolving from the subhuman stage, first began to possess tools and to use them consciously and deliberately to hunt and catch wild animals. This can be called the "hunting revolution," in contrast to the "agricultural revolution." One scholar has used the phrase "human revolution" to describe this revolution, since it was in this era that man evolved from the previous subhuman stage into a truly human being.

If we search for an equivalent revolution in patterns of living since the Industrial Revolution, we can certainly find it in this present age, namely, the revolution brought about by the development of atomic power. We are on the threshold of an age that future historians may refer to as the age of the "nuclear revolution."

Thus, we see that there have been, since men became human beings, several decisive turning points in the life of mankind. Limiting these to three, we cannot fail to note that, while the time span between the first revolution, the "hunting revolution," and the second, the "agricultural revolution," was hundreds of thousands of years, possibly over a million years, the time span between the completion of the "agricultural revolution" and the Industrial Revolution seems almost momentary, compared to the total expanse of human history. To us, several thousand years may seem very long, but the ten thousand years which lie between six to seven thousand years before Christ and the eighteenth century are but a moment in relation to the hundreds of thousands of years, perhaps a million years, before the historic era began. And during this time, in every region, arose the city civilizations of ancient times based upon the grain-raising agricultural revolution. The evolutionary process of the societies of ancient civilizations culminated in modern times in the revolution wrought in patterns of living by the Industrial Revolution. The time span between the Industrial Revolution and the beginning of the atomic age, what we might call the "nuclear revolution," is extremely short: after only about two hundred years or so we are facing another great turning point. When we consider this, it seems as if the progress of human culture, especially technological development within that culture, may be geometrical. These comments form a digression; what I wish to stress is that, when we think of Japanese history, we should place Yayoi culture or rice production within the context of these stages of world historical development.

In summary, the agricultural revolution, which had a decisive effect upon our lives, occurred in Japan around the beginning of the Christian era, constituting not only a revolution of grain-produc-

tion patterns but also a revolution involving a whole
series of skills essential to that pattern of living.
This agricultural revolution first began in Mesopotamia around 6000 to 7000 B.C., then reached
Egypt, the Indus River valley of India, and the
basin of the Yangtze River in China around 3000
B.C.

When we look at the entire Eurasian continent,
we see that the changes corresponding to the
agricultural revolution in Japan had already been
completed two or three thousand years before
they occurred in Japan, that is, at the earliest, several
thousand years ago.

The beginning of the Yayoi Age in Japan was
the time of the rise of the great Han Empire[1] in
China. The advanced civilization of the Han
Empire had already permeated the Korean peninsula. When we consider these trends in Asia, I find
it hard to accept the theory that the people of the
Jōmon period, through their own efforts, shifted
from a hunting economy to an agricultural economy
without any relation to developments on the Asian
continent, nor can I accept the idea that such a
theory will contribute to a scientific interpretation
of Japanese history. My own conclusion is that
grain production and irrigated rice cultivation,
with all the variety of new skills and patterns of
living that accompanied these, entered Japan after
having reached a stage of completion on the Asian
continent. As water flows from a higher to a lower
level, so a higher culture or civilization permeates
a lower. Since this is a recognizable trend in world
history, I think it is a matter of scholarly common
sense to assume that it was as a consequence of a
refined civilization flowing into Japan from neighboring China and Korea that a revolution in patterns
of life of such magnitude as the introduction of rice
production could have taken place.

1. 202 B.C. to A.D. 220, a period of
political and cultural expansion in
China. The Han dynasty defeated
the formidable Mongolian nomads, the Hsiung-nu, in the
north, conquered Korea in the
northeast, and extended the Chinese boundaries in the southwest.
Korean histories record that the
Japanese were established in Mimana on the southern coast of
Korea, and Japanese mythology
indicates that there was a close
connection between southern
Korea and western Japan. Archaeological remains of the Yayoi
period—wheelmade pottery and
bronzes made in Japan—provide
evidence of the increased continental influence resulting from
the Han expansion. Chinese
bronze mirrors, weapons, and
other continental imports have
been excavated from tombs in
northern Kyūshū belonging to the
middle Yayoi period, around the
beginning of the Christian era.

The Route of Transmission
of Rice Cultivation

2. *Kami-yo* or *Jindai*, the age of the gods, namely, the period recorded in Japanese mythology before the reign of the first emperor, Jimmu, 660–585 B.C., according to ancient tradition. *Kami-yo* is, therefore, the prehistoric period, the age of the shaman ruler. The shamanic diviner became ruler in the name of the *kami*, the gods or the spirits, and exercised a charismatic influence. Both the Shinto mythology and the account in the *Wajin-den* record the spiritual authority of the ruler who could become "*kami*-possessed." The Yamato dynasty claimed direct descent from Amaterasu, the Sun Goddess, which gave them imperial and priestly charisma. In his priestly office, the emperor communicated with Amaterasu, *kami* of the imperial clan. Queen Himiko of the Yamatai-koku described in the *Wajin-den* occupied herself with magic and sorcery.

3. 1881–1938. Hamada lectured on art history and archaeology at Kyoto University beginning in 1909 and conducted excavations of ancient tombs in South Manchuria and Korea during the period from 1910 to 1921. He was noted for his pioneering research on Chinese bronzes and artifacts, and for studies on Buddhist art and the Southern Barbarians.

The people of the Jōmon Age were nonliterate. It was once claimed that letters existed in the theocratic age,[2] but the Shinto priest who made this claim later admitted it to be a hoax. In any case, the people of the Jōmon Age did not have any writing system. How, then, did the nonliterate people of that age receive these new skills from the continent? Today it would be possible to learn new technology through the medium of books, television, or radio. Judging from what we know of the conditions of that age, however, it is unthinkable that rice production began as a result of knowledge transmitted solely from beyond the seas. Therefore, we must assume that continental peoples possessing knowledge of the new techniques of rice cultivation had contacts with the people of the Jōmon Age.

Exactly where did the new skills in living come from, then? Since irrigated rice production was not originally practiced in the north, it is unlikely that the new skills were transmitted from cold northern Asia. The areas for which there is proof of irrigated rice cultivation before the Yayoi Age lie to the south of the Japanese islands, that is, south of the Yangtze River, and in Honan. Lands farther south, that is, around the present North Vietnam, and, on the other hand, northern China may also have played a role, but the most significant regions were probably southern Korea and the Honan area, which are neighboring territories.

As for the route of transmission, one influential theory holds that it ran from southern Korea to northern Kyūshū, while Kōsaku Hamada[3] supports the theory that the techniques of rice production were transmitted from northern China (the former Manchuria) through the northern part of the Korean peninsula to southern Japan. On the basis of archaeological findings indicating that the distribution of the grain cutter spread northward, it is held that rice cultivation was transmitted from the north. However, there is no convincing evidence that irrigated rice cultivation was practiced from early times in northern China. There exist only a few clues pointing to traces of rice in the neolithic Yang-shao culture. In general, from historic times to the recent past, northern China, if a grain-producing region at all, was mainly a wheat-growing area.

In contrast to this, the region south of the Yangtze River has practiced rice cultivation from early times. As can be seen from the extent of the monsoon area covering Southeast Asia and south China, this part of the world has been divided from ancient times into two cultural spheres: the rice-growing region south of the Yangtze River and wheat-growing northern China. It would be more natural to assume that the northern grain cutter was used to cut ears of wheat, and that the similar grain cutter found south of the Yangtze was used to cut ears of rice. Further, the various newer semicircular agricultural tools, except the stone ax, are found in contiguous areas from south Korea to the southern part of the Chinese continent, rather than in the north. Consequently, the theory of the transmission of rice cultivation from the north is somewhat doubtful.

Kunio Yanagita's Interpretation

Here I would like to comment on Kunio Yanagita's *Kaijō no michi* [Sea routes] (volume 1 of *Teihon Yanagita Kunio shū* [Collected works of Kunio Yanagita], published by Chikuma Shobō, 1968). Yanagita placed emphasis on the sea currents that flow round the Japanese islands

from the south, i.e., the Tsushima Current, which
enters the Japan Sea from Okinawa, and the Black,
or Japan, Current, which moves northward along
the eastern seacoast of the Japanese islands. It was
along these two currents that the various cultures
from the islands to the south flowed into Japan.

However, I find it hard to accept Yanagita's
theory on the transmigration of a rice-growing
people who brought the agricultural revolution
to Japan: that it was a southern people who crossed
over to Japan by way of Okinawa. For me to
criticize Yanagita's theory would not, I think,
detract in any way from his greatness or from the
extent of his scholarship. There would be no
progress in learning if the succeeding generations
of scholars maintained as gospel the theories of any
particular scholar. Instead, the theories of any
scholar, however distinguished he may be, should
be gradually revised through the use of new materials and thus developed further. This is the way
scholarship advances.

Let me, then, raise some questions about
Yanagita's theory. Yanagita does not take a very
simple unilinear, monostructural approach to evolution, such as would maintain that Jōmon period
Japanese had invented new techniques entirely
within Japan and had advanced in this way from
a collecting and hunting economy to an agricultural
stage. Concerning the origins of the Japanese,
Yanagita, with poetic intuition maintained throughout his life, envisaged a transmigration of a rice-
raising people through Okinawa. However, he
had an extremely negative attitude toward the
findings of archaeologists, and this is the problem.

When a specialized course on cultural anthropology was established at the University of Tokyo
over ten years ago, I took about ten students
majoring in cultural anthropology in the Department of Cultural Studies to Yanagita's home, so
they could have a chance to listen to him. On that

occasion too, Yanagita talked enthusiastically about his theory of sea routes. He declared in effect that one cannot rely on archaeologists. Traces of rice husks on the bottom of pots are surely accidental, he said, for "there is no reason why rice should deliberately approach pots and stick to them." Even if by some chance rice husks had stuck to pots, however, this would be no indication of the beginning of rice cultivation. When one considers Japanese culture, he said, it is probable that rice cultivation is far older than the Yayoi Age. Thus Yanagita earnestly argued along these lines; his ideas are clearly expressed in his writings.

Yet, the more archaeological evidence continues to accumulate, the more untenable this view becomes. Even if Jōmon pottery bearing traces of rice husks were discovered, I think this would indicate merely the prelude to the beginning of the Yayoi Age, the introduction of rice culture in the latest period of the Jōmon Age. In the Yayoi Age, at least in western Japan, we may conclude, on the basis of the available material evidence, that there occurred a marked change of an alien nature in all aspects of life, as compared with the previous Jōmon Age. If we take this as a clue to the origins of the Japanese people, then the relationship of the archaeological materials on Yayoi culture to the neighboring areas around Japan becomes an important problem.

Although I am not an archaeologist, it seems to me that the theory that the Yayoi culture entered Japan from Okinawa, so that even today a primitive type of Japanese culture remains in Okinawa, is difficult to maintain from the archaeological standpoint. It appears rather that Yayoi culture was formed first in Japan, after which it spread south to Okinawa. This is why ancient customs and ancient beliefs that have since undergone great changes in the Japanese islands have been preserved in Okinawa to the present day. This view too re-

quires further archaeological investigation, however.

The Transmission of Rice Cultivation from South Korea

Consequently, there emerges the following
archaeological problem. Which of the regions that
had already become a rice-raising cultural sphere
in the pre-Yayoi period was the closest to Japan?
We can only conclude that this region was the
southern half of the Korean peninsula, that is,
the present Republic of Korea. We may even
consider that, for a time, southern Korea and
western Japan formed a closely related cultural
sphere that was almost a single unit. From archaeological remains, we may conclude that the
beginnings of rice production came about two
centuries earlier in southern Korea than in Japan.

In Japan, Yayoi pottery[4] has been thoroughly
discussed, and among Japanese archaeologists the
dominant view is that there still has not been
confirmation of the existence in southern Korea
of pottery corresponding to Yayoi pottery, and
that Yayoi pottery has many distinctively Japanese
features, especially those which show continuity
with Jōmon pottery,[5] so it would be premature
to relate Yayoi culture to south Korea solely on
the basis of pottery. Recently, however, at the
Karakuri site near the Han River close to Seoul,
discoveries have been made of pottery identical
with Yayoi pottery. In Korea this is the type called
red plain pottery. It has not yet been classified and
organized into types in such great numbers as in
Japan, but it seems that, in the field of pottery too,
the connection between Yayoi culture and southern
Korea will be clarified before long.

Further, when we view this within the context
of cultural history, it is not only the shape of the

4. Yayoi pottery was generally
wheelmade, limited to fewer
shapes than Jōmon pottery,
reddish in color, and thin. Surface
decoration included painted
designs, scratching, and combing.

5. Cord-marking or cord impressions were used to decorate the
surface of Jōmon pottery. In fact,
the word Jōmon means "cord
impression." This ceramic art was
of great variety and beauty. One
of its products was a spouted jar,
the forerunner of the teapot. "Today's omnipresent Japanese teapot
has a four thousand year heritage"
(J. Edward Kidder, *Japan before
Buddhism* [rev. ed.; New York:
Praeger, 1966], p. 66). No pot-
ter's wheel appears to have been
used.

pottery but also the techniques of livelihood practiced in the Yayoi Age, the whole complex of patterns of living, that concern us. It is not merely rice cultivation or pottery, the individual cultural elements, but the combination of these which interacts to form the whole of a people's way of life that concerns us. From this point of view, the basically agricultural form of living found in southern Korea from about 500 B.C. to around the beginning of the Christian era has a great many elements in common with the life of the agricultural people of the Yayoi Age in Japan.

Moreover, in Korea each item of technology spread a stage earlier than in Japan. It is very likely that influences from the cultural sphere of the Chinese continent entered earlier into the Korean peninsula, which is geographically closer to China. Metallurgy, weaving, various techniques of wood carving, also the techniques of making pottery fired at a much higher temperature than Jōmon pottery —all of these entered Korea earlier than Japan. In regard to Okinawa, however, we have no archaeological remains corresponding to these.

It will be clear from the above that, when we consider from which direction Yayoi culture entered Japan, we must assume the existence of a continuous cultural zone extending from southern Korean rice-growing regions to western Japan. The various agricultural tools excavated in Korea which I have mentioned and the polished stone implements which appear to have been used in wood carving have a great deal in common with those found in Japan. Further, tools dating from the early to the middle periods of the Tomb Age and identical with those made earlier in Korea have been excavated in Japan.

Susumu Ohno of Gakushūin University, in his book *Nihongo no kigen* [Origins of the Japanese language], has attempted to support this theory from the viewpoint of language. Ohno points out the similarities between the Japanese and Korean words concerning the fundamental skills and crafts of daily life that presumably spread through Japan together with rice cultivation in the Yayoi Age. He has listed and compared agriculture-related words in Japanese and Korean, such as "field" or "hoe," as well as words related to household or village skills, such as "silk" or "loom," and has found examples of correspondence in sounds. Some scholars have criticized specific examples in the list as inappropriate, but I think at least a few of the cases cited by Ohno are ones that any scholar would respect.

My own theory about the route whereby Japanese rice cultivation, or Yayoi culture, which formed the basic culture of the Japanese people, was transmitted is neither that of the route through north China, Manchuria, and Korea, nor the theory advanced by Yanagita in *Kaijō no michi*. When it comes to the question of how rice cultivation reached southern Korea, however, my own ideas come close to those of Yanagita.

In any consideration of this question, the great problem is finally the region south of the Yangtze River. I myself would trace the route of the transmission of rice cultivation to southern Korea from the river basin of the Yangtze River through the East China Sea, skirting the Shantung Peninsula to southern Korea. Many scholars hold this view, and various proofs have been offered.

The idea that rice cultivation was an indigenous invention might win support if there existed at present a wild species of Japanese rice, or if there were any evidence that such a species had existed in the past, but so far no evidence of this kind has been brought forward. It is said that the variety of Japanese rice called *Oryza sativa japonica* has been the rice cultivated in Japan from the Yayoi Age down to the present day, and this species was originally grown in central China and along the eastern seaboard of south China. Scholarly proof of this has been produced by Yanagita and by specialists such as Hirotaro Andō,[6] his collaborator.

In addition, Nobuhiro Matsumoto[7] of Keio University has for a long time emphasized the continuity between Yayoi culture and Southeast Asia and south China through a comparison of languages and of diverse aspects of folklore, rituals, and customs which accompany rice cultivation.

There are various theories regarding the origin of the Japanese word for rice, *ine*, but the *n* sound cannot be considered a Chinese sound. The fact that *nep*, *ni*, and *nun*, similar sounds, are to be found in the Indonesian family of languages ranging from south China to Southeast Asia has been given as evidence for this.

Through these data drawn from every aspect of archaeology and linguistics, it may be judged that the rice-growing culture extending from southern Korea to western Japan—not rice growing itself, but the cultural complex based on rice growing—was also that of the people living south of the Yangtze River, whom the people of Han regarded as aliens and called Southern Barbarians.

The Yayoi culture was, as explained above, formed on the basis of the agricultural revolution achieved through the transmission of rice cultivation from the region south of the Yangtze River through southern Korea to Japan. A phenomenon similar to that which arose in Japan after the Meiji era when the waves of the Western Industrial Revolution overwhelmed Japan began in this Yayoi Age. In this way Yayoi culture, spreading first in western Japan, permeated the Japanese islands by degrees, moving in a northeasterly direction. This would be the consensus of Japanese scholars. Therefore, the Yayoi culture of the northeast region began

6. 1871–1958. Doctor of Agriculture, former head of the National Agricultural Experiment Station, and founder of the study of agriculture in Japan. Andō conducted research on prevention of cold-weather damage to crops and is known for his contributions to the improvement of species of rice, and his studies on the history of rice in ancient Japan.

7. 1897—. Historian and ethnologist of Indochina. His works cover Japanese mythology, ancient Japanese history, and Indian and Chinese culture.

much later than that of western Japan, and in Hokkaidō rice production was probably almost unknown until the Meiji period.

Thus far, my consideration of the formation of Yayoi culture has been based on the assumption that a new people transmitted the seeds of an agricultural revolution to Japan. For I think that the formation of Yayoi culture cannot be considered unless we assume there was such a transmigration of people of a cultural sphere alien to Japan, or some contact with such people. Thus arises the problem of who these people were.

The People Who Brought Rice Cultivation to Japan

Did a great folk migration to Japan take place in the Yayoi Age, driving out or completely assimilating the Jōmon people? One line of reasoning would be to conjecture that the contemporaneous Chinese had named the people undertaking this great migration the Wa people. But such surmises cannot be lightly made. In any case, the beginning of the Yayoi Age can be placed around the second or third century before Christ. In order better to understand this period, let us take a brief look at the conditions on the Asian continent at that time.

On the Asian continent, the Chou period[8] was ending, and consolidation under the Han began after the Ch'in-Han age. The country was unified by the first emperor of Ch'in,[9] who built the Great Wall of China and the palace celebrated in the "Ode on the Afang Palace" by the poet Tu Mu[10] in the lines "The Six States end,[11] the four seas become one, bare mountains of Szechwan loom beyond, and Afang emerges." Eventually disorder and chaos brought about the downfall of the Ch'in

8. c. 1122–249 B.C. Interstate warfare took place after 771 B.C., the date that divides West Chou (c. 1122–771 B.C.) from East Chou (770–249 B.C.); during the latter period, China developed schools of thought that formed the basic attitudes toward the universe and patterns of social and political organization that persisted into the twentieth century, and also influenced Korea and Japan. Under the Chou, the ruler was looked upon as the son of T'ien (Heaven), and the concepts of T'ien and the Shang Ti (the Shang term for the Supreme Being) coalesced. The main school of philosophy was Confucianism, which gave China and her neighboring countries the ideals of good government and a code of ethics. Among the other schools of thought, the most influential was that of Taoism. Divination based on the concepts of *yin* and *yang* was transmitted in the *I ching*, or Book of Changes, with the other classics that embodied the philosophies of this era.

9. Ch'in Shih Huang-Ti, 259–210 B.C. (Ch'in dynasty, 221–207 B.C.). The Ch'in, a people from the northwest, unified China under the leadership of Prince Cheng, who subsequently took the title Shih Huang-Ti (first emperor) and established a centralized system.

10. A.D. 803–852. A Chinese poet and painter of the T'ang period.

11. A reference to the six states of China—Han, Chao, Wei, Ch'u, Yen, and Ch'i—rivals of the state of Ch'in, which finally conquered them all in 230–221 B.C.

Empire,[12] and the age of the Han-Ch'u war story began: the struggle between the founder of the Han dynasty and Hsiang Yü[13] of Ch'u took place, resulting in unification of the land under the former. Then the civilization of the Han Empire spread throughout Asia. All these events occurred in the period from 300 B.C. onward. The confusion of the whole land in the latter part of the Chou period had preceded this, and there were great disturbances among the neighboring peoples living on the frontiers of China, accompanied by migrations of peoples surrounding the Han people.

The activities of the northern nomadic peoples, the horse-riding peoples, are often mentioned in the histories of this age, and the activities of the Huns are well known. The migrations in the region south of the Yangtze River were undoubtedly connected with the confusion at the end of the Chou age. There might very well have been a migration of a people whose culture was based on rice cultivation from the region south of the Yangtze River through China and across the East China Sea to southern Korea.

In spite of the lack of detailed information about the changes in and formations of peoples in southern Korea, we may conjecture that there was a continuing wave of migrations of people who transmitted a rice-growing culture from southern Korea crossing the Tsushima Straits into Japan. It is at this point that the people of the Jōmon Age pose a problem. The Jōmon culture existed in regions toward the east rather than the west of Japan. Almost certainly this Jōmon culture was developed by men who conducted a fairly stable settled life based from early times on a hunting and food-gathering economy which involved fishing for salmon and trout along river banks and the seacoast, catching shellfish, and hunting deer and boar in the mountains. Unless there were settled communi-

12. 221–207 B.C. Ch'in, the first dynasty to unify China, gave its name to the land.

13. 233–202 B.C. The collapse of the Ch'in dynasty brought on a struggle for power between the rival military leaders Hsiang Yü and Liu Pang. Hsiang Yü was destroyed by Liu Pang, who founded the dynasty.

ties, such pottery as the elaborate and intricately decorated Jōmon pottery could not possibly have been made. It is a general rule that pottery is not made by nomadic peoples, or hunting peoples without a settled habitation. A nomadic people will make vessels from the skins of domestic animals and preserve food or water in them, while a hunting people will make vessels out of the bark of trees. Even today, in north Asia, vessels made from the bark of the white birch tree are used, but no pottery is made.

In the latter part of the Jōmon Age, plants other than the rice plant, e.g., some root crops, may have been cultivated, but the great characteristic of the Jōmon culture was ultimately a life sustained by a food-gathering economy consisting of gathering, hunting, and fishing. Furthermore, it can be surmised from the pottery of the era that the Jōmon Age culture was one in which the techniques of a food-gathering economy were developed to their highest level. Of course, the size of the shell mounds also testifies to this, but our deepest interest lies in the Jōmon pottery.

What became of the Jōmon Age people in the later periods of Japanese history—these people who made pottery of such a high level of craftsmanship and beauty, judged from the point of view of both cultural and art history? For it seems most unlikely that the people who left us the Jōmon pottery should have disappeared soon after the beginning of the Yayoi Age.

Particularly as the Yayoi culture spread from west to east along the Japanese islands, this change from the Jōmon to the Yayoi was not a sudden qualitative change, but rather one in which characteristics of the Yayoi pottery became conspicuous within the Jōmon tradition. Thus, scholars who study the archaeology of the northwest maintain that the change from Jōmon to Yayoi constituted not a "revolution" but "evolution." In their judgment it was the Jōmon Age people who made Yayoi pottery and practiced rice cultivation. At least in regard to eastern Japan, this theory carries relative weight. Though it is difficult to offer a generally acceptable theory, I can introduce one or two well-known theories such as the following.

Takeo Kanazeki,[14] a specialist in the study of human skeletons in relation to anthropology, has measured the rather large number of human bones found in Yayoi sites in western Japan and as a result has published the following findings. The average height of the Yayoi man of these sites had at one time rapidly become taller than that of the Jōmon man of the previous age. The calculations further reveal that afterward the average height became progressively lower until finally it was so low that it was not much different from the height of the Jōmon man. Kanazeki's interpretation is that in the beginning the average height of Yayoi man grew rapidly in comparison with the Jōmon man of that area because a tall people bringing the new techniques of rice cultivation had moved from southern Korea to western Japan; this influence, he contends, may perhaps be seen in the skeletal remains of these people. At any rate, the average height of the Jōmon people had temporarily grown taller through the influence of this people. But the population of the people who had migrated was far smaller than that of the aboriginal Jōmon people. Thus, in time, the attribute of greater height was absorbed through intermarriage with the aboriginal stock of Jōmon people, and eventually it disappeared. Although his assumptions are based on the results of an investigation of only one specific region, Kanazeki arrived at the above general interpretation.

If his theory is correct, there would also have been a large residue of the language of the Jōmon people of western Japan embedded in the language

14. 1897—. Kanazeki has written on the origins of mankind and on the ancient Far East.

of the people who were later known as the Wa. The alien people who possessed the new techniques of rice production were such a minority that they were absorbed through intermarriage into the aboriginal Jōmon people. Moreover, the language of the Yayoi people was not basically different in linguistic structure from that of the Jōmon people, so that we may consider the language of the Jōmon people as forming the basis of the language of the later Japanese. Thus, the further back we move in time, the more difficult it is to make assumptions and the more tenuous our premises become.

Considerations Based on Linguistics

The philologist Susumu Ohno, whose theory I cited previously, also believes that a people bringing a rice-growing culture to Japan moved along the route I have mentioned. The premise of his hypothesis is the language of the people who possessed this culture and migrated from the region south of the Yangtze River in the troubled period of Chinese history. To summarize Ohno's hypothesis, first, the language of a certain people who migrated from south of the Yangtze River to southern Korea became assimilated into the northern Altaic language structure. This was the ancestral form of the Korean language and was almost the same as the speech of the ancient Koreans. Then, people who spoke this language together with the new Yayoi culture spread to western Japan, where the former inhabitants, the Jōmon Age people, were already settled. Thus there was formed a mixture of the speech of the ancient Koreans who spread in Japan, a language structurally Altaic, and the speech of the Jōmon people. This mixture was the speech of the people of Wa, probably the original form of the Japanese language. Such is the explanation offered by Ohno. Thus, the people of Wa and the ancient Koreans were very closely related and their patterns of living had much in common, but their languages diverged rather markedly even from this age, so that the Chinese probably distinguished between the ancient Koreans and the Wa people as two different peoples.

Ohno's theory is based on the tentative premise that in grammatical structure the Japanese language belongs to the Altaic family of languages. Therefore, it follows that the people who brought rice cultivation to Japan were already speaking a language with a grammatical structure of Altaic lineage, and that the speech of the alien people determined the basic structure of the later Japanese language.

Further, Ohno held that the language spoken by the Jōmon people had the Southern Austric characteristic of all syllables ending in vowels, rather than Northern Altaic characteristics. Peoples who speak languages with syllables ending in vowels are spread across the southern sector of the South Pacific, including, for instance, Polynesia and Hawaii. Thus, according to Ohno's theory, the present Japanese language was formed by the superimposition of an Altaic structure on the language of southern lineage spoken by the Jōmon people.

Of course, Ohno's hypothesis has encountered various criticisms from other philologists, whose viewpoints should also be studied. The reason I have taken up Ohno's theory along with that of Kanazeki, the anthropologist, is that Ohno's hypothesis emphasizes even more strongly than Kanazeki's the relative weight of the immigrant people who brought the Yayoi culture to Japan.

Thus, it is not easy to offer incontrovertible evidence about the history and character of this age. To determine the origins of a language is an especially difficult problem. In criticizing Ohno's theory, Shirō Hattori,[15] following orthodox linguistics, raises the following objections. First, Hattori points out that, as a general rule, it is impossible for two languages to mix and form a new, third language. When two different languages come in contact and mix, the usual result is that one of the languages predominates or drives out the other, and it is unheard of for a new language to be formed out of a mixture of the two languages.

However, in answer to my inquiry, Ohno stated that, to date, linguistic theories have been based upon the standard of the languages of the Indo-European peoples, which have had an extremely strong tendency to subjugate other languages. It is true that when the Indo-European peoples have conquered alien peoples, no mixed language has emerged. Invariably the speech of the conquering Indo-European peoples has prevailed. However, Ohno mentions that no evidence has been offered from the history of the intermingling of peoples other than Indo-Europeans; thus, the question whether or not a mixed language has ever emerged has yet to be answered.

In the history of the conquests of the Indo-European peoples, for instance when the Aryans entered India and conquered the natives, the Aryan language, which belongs to the same family of languages as the various European languages, dominated the languages of the Indians. On the American continents, the languages of the white peoples who conquered the indigenous Indians have become dominant: in North America, English; in Latin America, Spanish and Portuguese. On visiting a village in Mexico, we may find many people who are bilingual, speaking Spanish as well as the Aztec or Mayan language for instance, but even if people speak two languages there is no case of the two blending and a third, new language emerging.

15. 1908—. A linguistics scholar, Hattori has published studies on linguistic methodology, and the origins of the Japanese language based upon the glotto-chronological methodology of M. Swadish.

As is illustrated by the above, the task of producing evidence of the formation of a mixed language in the history of linguistic contacts is formidable. Yet there is abundant evidence of mixtures in aspects of culture other than language and in physiognomy. In religion—although Islam offers extremely few examples of mixing with other religions—from very early times in Japan a mixture of Buddhism and Shinto was very readily practiced. In short, it is still a great unsolved question whether language is the only cultural element that does not permit mixtures.

The Yayoi Age as a Formative Period for the Japanese People

However, the Ohno theory also contains many other doubtful points. For instance, there is the question whether the Jōmon culture, which lasted for several thousand years, was that of a single people. Perhaps several different types of peoples scattered in different parts of the Japanese islands pursued the same kind of food-gathering economy. Also, it was a widely accepted theory in the Meiji era that the Ainu[16] were a Jōmon Age people, but this too is doubtful, for it can also be argued that the Ainu are a later people who did not exist in the Jōmon Age.

Again, anthropologists surmise that, if the Jōmon people were not Ainu, the present-day Japanese are the descendants of these early non-Ainu people. But is there any proof for this view either?

Further, during the Jōmon Age, there may have been various migrations of peoples and transmission, influence, or mixtures of cultures in different periods. There are still mysteries; some may be solved and some may remain permanently unknown. In any case, the culture and language of the people of the Jōmon Age, who left evidence of a

16. The origin of the Ainu, a minority ethnic group in Japan, is still the subject of controversy. Many anthropologists hold that they are a Caucasoid group because of their light skin color, wavy hair, and heavy body hair. It is estimated that there were about 10,000 Ainu in the early 1960s and, because of intermarriage with the Japanese, only a few hundred of them were full-blooded members of their race. Originally they pursued a hunting and food-gathering economy. The Ainu language differs from the Japanese, and efforts are being made to preserve the epics handed down through their oral tradition. Since the Meiji period, the Japanese government has passed various laws aimed at assimilating the Ainu.

fairly prosperous life throughout practically the entire area of the Japanese archipelago, were surely not unrelated to the people of Wa, that is, the Japanese of the historic period, or to the formation of the Japanese people, or to the sources of Japanese culture.

Among the scholars who are attempting to reconstruct history from the ethnological point of view, some consider that the taro[17] or yam—a kind of root crop—which corresponds to the Japanese potato, *sato-imo*, grown in the south of Japan, was cultivated in Japan in the Jōmon Age. Even today, in certain scattered regions of Japan, there survive rituals involving the use of the *imo* at the festival of the full moon and at other festivals. Some hold the view that the customs of the Jōmon Age, which developed before the introduction of rice cultivation, were displaced by the rice-growing rituals that accompanied the later spread of rice cultivation, so that the former survived only in the inaccessible mountain regions of western Japan. Of course, this is possible. However, the lack of archaeological evidence makes it equally possible to argue that the *imo* was introduced into Japan together with rice, or after the Yayoi Age. Moreover, even if cultivation of *imo* was transmitted to Japan in the Yayoi Age or later, there is ample possibility that it would naturally have spread, skipping over the rice-growing areas, in the distant mountain regions unsuited for Japanese wet rice cultivation, so that in such regions not rice but *imo* rituals might be performed both now and then. This is a very perverse argument, but unless a counterargument can be put forward to demonstrate its implausibility, those who are familiar with my theories may not easily be convinced.

I myself would like to refrain here from making this kind of conjecture. I do not deny that the culture of the Jōmon people left the succeeding people of Wa a great tradition. At the same time, I have

17. The edible root of a stemless, araceous plant grown in tropical regions.

not ignored the fact that the beauty of Jōmon pottery has made its mark in the art history of the Japanese people, and that often in later periods this type of beauty has been reevaluated and reemphasized.

However, according to my initial definition, the people we can objectively call the Japanese people were first formed in these islands during the Yayoi Age, when there occurred a series of technological revolutions based upon the cultivation of rice in paddy fields, accompanied by a sudden rapid increase in population. Many scholars have already concluded from archaeological remains that, as the Jōmon Age passed into the Yayoi Age, there was a great increase in the population of Japan.

My own conclusion is that the Yayoi Age, around the beginning of the Christian era, was the age during which an agricultural revolution took place in Japan, the population increased suddenly, and the Chinese chronicles recorded the existence of a people who presumably spoke Japanese, in other words, the age in which there first came to exist a people we can clearly identify as Japanese. Should one trace the sources of the ethnic traits of the Japanese, or the basic characteristics of the Japanese culture—what may be called the "patterns" of Japanese culture—in all probability they would be found in the Yayoi Age.

This is a broad sketch, but in my own opinion it is a view that is relatively consistent, and I suspect that any view that assumes more than this lacks scholarly persuasiveness. My own explanation, on the other hand, is quite acceptable within the limits of present-day knowledge.

The Yayoi Age eventually developed into the Tomb Age. In my opinion, the age of Queen Himiko[18] of the Yamatai country falls at the end of the Yayoi Age or perhaps in the early period of the Tomb Age. Also, it is fairly clear that a certain

18. Queen Himiko is discussed more fully in Chap. 4.

period of the Tomb Age witnessed the historical unification of the land by the Yamato dynasty, the ancestors of the present Japanese imperial family. This theme I shall discuss in the next chapter, "The Origins of the Japanese State."

4.   The Origins of the Japanese State

The Administration of the Village Community

Let us now consider, in the light of the sources of the Japanese culture, the problem of the origins of the Japanese state. I shall treat the people and the state as two different concepts and deal with their origins separately. However, in making a comprehensive study of problems such as Japanese culture in the widest sense, or the formation of Japanese culture, or the national character or ethnic traits of the Japanese people, the issue of the origins of the state should be treated as part of the problem of the origins of the people and of the culture. With this in mind, I have spent some time going back to the sources of the Japanese people.

As I related in the previous chapter, it is the Yayoi Age as defined by archaeologists—namely, the age of the Wa people recorded in the ancient books of China—which we can identify as the earliest source of evidence that allows us to distinguish our ancestors. During this entire age, the superior continental civilization was transmitted in fluctuating waves through the Korean peninsula to Japan. Of course, it may be taken for granted that the knowledge of metal implements and the techniques of metallurgy developed in this age were introduced from the continent.

Judging from archaeological remains and sites, one characteristic of this age was that in general there was very little militarism. The ornaments found in burial mounds are largely ceremonial jewels or mirrors, and a great many of the swords and halberds too are ceremonial rather than designed for practical use. There are few sites in which the communities have ditches or walls surrounding them for defense purposes, and, in effect, the nature of the culture seems to have been markedly peaceful, agrarian, and ceremonial.

The details of life are obscure, but throughout this age small village communities existed, probably at first scattered here and there. Eventually, as agricultural life developed, it would have been difficult for small communities to maintain complete economic self-sufficiency. This is clear from a survey of world history. Once an agricultural revolution has been achieved through the introduction of grain cultivation, and a society of settled agricultural villages develops, small communities come to be linked together in various ways through common pursuits. In particular, as technology advanced, it would have become increasingly difficult for an isolated community to undertake the labor necessary for irrigation of paddy fields. Inevitably the demand would arise for corporate administration of waterways which pass through several communities. Further, religious leadership would emerge to consolidate the village communities for some common purpose. In the beginning the leader probably was not a military figure but a religious and ceremonial leader who emerged to undertake the common administration of such communities. In various countries at this stage of settled agricultural village life, there were rather large buildings in which common religious rituals for several village communities were held. Even today, many monuments of stone or clay remain in certain regions of Mesopotamia, Egypt, the Andes, and Latin America. Yet in Japan, perhaps because of the building materials used, the

existence in this age of such huge structures corresponding to "ceremonial centers" has not been
proved. Instead of this, we find the appearance of
burial mounds made by heaping up the earth,
which must have required the use of considerable
labor. This, I think, supports my line of reasoning,
as I have explained it thus far.

From Ceremonial Communities to Military Communities

Eventually, as a general trend in world history,
the religious leader took on a leading role in
economic and political institutions as well. Under
these circumstances, the scattered ceremonial centers developed into small theocratic chiefdoms
and grew into regional powers. In time, conflicting
interests arose among these regional powers and
they began to acquire military traits. There is
evidence of this process in Japan. At the same time,
sites and relics show how all societies that developed
from settled agricultural villages into ancient states,
especially those in areas where ancient civilizations
arose, went through a similar process. They
gradually evolved from peaceful communities
predominantly religious in character into communities that possessed arms or fortresses. This seems
to have been a general historical pattern in ancient
times throughout the world.

In Japan, too, the period just preceding the Tomb
Age, and probably the conditions of the various
chiefdoms or states of Wa around the third century
of the Christian era, as described in the *Wajin-den*,
represented such a stage of development. At the
end of the Yayoi Age or the beginning of the
Tomb Age, the Yamatai-koku, Kuna-koku, and
others, that is, the large and small thirty-odd
kingdoms of the people of Wa recorded in the

Wajin-den, were probably at the stage when a theocratic order was just beginning to acquire militaristic aspects.

If we turn to the process of the accession to the throne of Queen Himiko of Yamatai-koku, according to the record in the *Wajin-den*, Wa was in turmoil, and civil war continued for several years. After this, all the people together enthroned a woman. Now this woman, Queen Himiko, had a strongly theocratic and ceremonial character. It is recorded that she practiced sorcery and troubled the people, so we can surmise that Himiko had magic functions and stood at the apex of a theocratic government.

Again, after the death of Himiko, it is recorded that over a hundred servants were sacrificed and for this purpose a large burial mound was erected. It is not possible now to know whether or not this account is exaggerated. However, we may conjecture that in the Wa state of the early Tomb Age, burial mounds were erected for powerful persons in this way and human sacrifice was practiced.

There is also a passage relating that after the death of the powerful Himiko there was again discontent and civil war in the kingdom, and over a thousand persons were killed. Thus, in this age there were probably rivalries and wars between local powers.

Now in regard to our theme, the origins of the Japanese state, it is usually held that, out of the feuds between these local powers, the various states of the people of Wa arose here and there in western Japan, and from their struggles the power referred to in the *Wajin-den* as Yamatai-koku came to consolidate western Japan, establishing the Yamato dynasty of historical record. If this Yamatai-koku is indeed Yamato, and if one could thus interpret Japanese history by dating the hegemony of the Yamato dynasty from this point, it would be a very simple matter indeed, but such an interpretation cannot be made so easily.

The Nature and Periodization of the Tomb Age

Within the age designated by archaeologists as the Tomb Age, the early period, as pointed out by scholars who define it as the late Yayoi Age, shows continuity with the cultural character of the ceremonial Yayoi Age. This continuity is clear from archaeological sites and relics. However, while some theories divide the Tomb Age into two periods, early and late, other theories divide it into three: early, middle, and late. In fact, up till now, most books have used the triple division. If we follow this system provisionally, the early age would extend from the third century, when the tombs and mounded graves began to appear, through a period of change and into the fourth century, ending roughly in the latter part of that century; it would cover less than a century. This early period, extending into the fourth century, is a period in which the Yayoi tradition was still conspicuous. The late period is a fairly long one, extending from the middle of the fifth century up to the Asuka age of the seventh century, and in the latter part of the late period we begin to find historical documents. This is clearly the period of what is known in history as the establishment of the Yamato court. Consequently, the mounded graves of the later period are those of the aristocracy surrounding the Yamato court or of local chieftains. I think no scholar would disagree with this.

However, the middle period of the triple division is very controversial. As a result of the cumulative research of Japanese historians, what we may take as the generally accepted interpretation identifies the middle period of the Tomb Age as covering

1. The Chinese chronicle of the early sixth century, the *Liu Sung shu*, records tribute received from five Japanese emperors whose Chinese-style recorded names have been the basis for identification with the Yamato emperors described in the *Kojiki* and *Nihon-shoki*, the sixteenth emperor (Nintoku) or the seventeenth (Richū) to the twenty-first (Yūryaku). Ōjin, the father of Nintoku, is undoubtedly a historical ruler, since the two Japanese chronicles show a clear distinction in their narratives between accounts of the preceding rulers up to and including the reign of the empress Jingū, the mother of Ōjin, and those of Ōjin and his successors. The narratives of the earlier period are largely myths centering around the formation and evolution of the Japanese state, whereas those of the later period deal mainly with the rivalries of court factions and tales of hunting and feasting.

A theory has been put forward that the emperor Ōjin had been the founder of a new dynasty. Mitsusada Inoue (see n. 7, below) supports this on the grounds that the Japanese chronicles state that Ōjin married into the Yamato dynasty, and that he was born in Kyūshū. Ōjin was probably a territorial magnate of Kyūshū who later conquered the Yamato court. According to Inoue, Ōjin's reign was known for the unification of the state and the invasion of Korea (though the two Japanese chronicles attribute the latter to the empress Jingū).

2. A.D. 304–439. A period during which five major Mongolian and other related tribes invaded north China and established sixteen kingdoms, some of which lasted only a few years. These nomadic peoples became Sinicized, and Buddhism spread in China during this period.

the end of the fourth century and the beginning of the fifth century, roughly half a century. This corresponds to the reigns of the historical emperors Ōjin and Nintoku. Research supporting this interpretation has focused on the correspondence between the names of the Wa kings in the Chinese chronicles and the names of the emperors in the *Nihon-shoki*, and the period from about the fourth to the fifth century has been thought to cover the reigns of Ōjin and Nintoku. Also, a study of the proper nouns appearing in the Chinese chronicles has made it fairly clear that their reigns fall within this period.[1]

At about this time, judging from archaeological evidence, the transition from the early to the middle periods took place. Again, in this period, there was a great change in the funerary objects of the burial mounds: from the mirrors, jewels, and swords of the ceremonial and magic tradition since the Yayoi Age to practical and military weapons or horse-trappings, or stone replicas of daily utensils. This change began at the end of the fourth century and can be clearly traced in the fifth century.

The change is thought to be due to certain alien elements appearing in Japan at that time, bringing about the transformation of the culture from a ceremonial to a military one. Moreover, most of these weapons or horse-trappings and accessories appear after the collapse of the great Han Empire. There was confusion and turmoil among the neighboring peoples of China during the collapse of the Han, from the third to the fifth centuries. This is a recurrent pattern in Far Eastern history. After the fall of the Han Empire, during the period of the Five Tribes-Sixteen Kingdoms,[2] to the north of China nomadic peoples established many small states in succession. These states absorbed a great deal of Chinese culture yet preserved their own equestrian life and cavalry tactics. This was the period in which the so-called Hu[3] were active on the northern borders of China.

This was also the period when various accessories, weapons, and horse-trappings, bearing the culture of the Hu, appeared in Japan. These objects, of course, appeared in Korea long before they were found in Japan. If we examine the horse-trappings, the costumes, and the accessories of the warriors of that time in Korean museums and compare them with those of the years after the middle period of the Tomb Age, we find that some are indistinguishable. In other words, it is clear at a glance that the northern equestrian culture entered Japan by way of the Korean peninsula. The shining golden accouterments of the continental aristocrat, from headgear to footwear, have been found in Japan inside mounds dating from the fifth century. This has also been discussed by the archaeologist Yukio Kobayashi.[4]

During this period, on the Korean peninsula, the Koguryo or Puyo,[5] who possessed this equestrian culture, moved south from the northern areas and established states. Historians acknowledge that these peoples had markedly equestrian characteristics. On the other hand, in Japan during the same period unprecedented, great burial mounds such as the tombs of Ōjin and Nintoku, the ground areas of which are larger than those of the Egyptian pyramids, began to be built.

In time, various characteristics thought to be continental in origin appeared in Japanese burial practices. The mounds of the corridor type, or the stone chambers with mural paintings which have recently been discovered in Kyūshū and have aroused controversy, show clearly the influence of a culture that can be traced through Korea to the north. These changes represent the great characteristics of the transition from the early to the middle period of the Tomb Age.

3. Northern nomadic peoples. After the rise of the Hsiung-nu (Huns) toward the end of the third century before Christ, the terms Hsiung-nu and Hu were used as synonyms. However, during and after the Han period, the peoples east of the Pamir (a mountainous region in central Asia) were referred to as Western Hu or sometimes merely Hu.

4. 1911—. Kobayashi, lecturer of Kyoto University, has written several volumes on the Tomb Age.

5. The Koguryo were a branch of the Puyo, an eastern Manchurian people. They were a hunting people who, after bitter conflict with China, created a state extending over much of Manchuria and Korea by the fourth century.

Interpreting the Evidence
of the Transition

No scholar would deny the fact that very great changes took place during this period, but their interpretations of these changes differ. One interpretation, based on a purely archaeological viewpoint, holds that the Wa people described by the Chinese chronicles may have spread in western Japan or even farther south, but that they also occupied the southern part of the Korean peninsula. This interpretation results from the following line of reasoning.

Suppose that the sphere of influence of the Wa people extended from the west of Japan to a corner of southern Korea. One of the local governments or powers among these Japanese, either through contact with the culture of the northern equestrian people who had gradually moved south since the times of the ascendancy of the Koguryo and Puyo, or through assimilation of this type of culture, suddenly became a military power, erected a military state there, and unified Japan. This was the origin of the Japanese state.

Such an interpretation is acceptable, as it lies within the boundaries of available archaeological data. However, there are some strange facts that cannot be fully explained by this interpretation alone. Several mysteries remain, and their solution is a challenge to the cultural historian. These are the factors that led to the equestrian people theory, which I shall now explain. I will try to describe this theory objectively, in the way that I dealt with the theory of the agricultural people. As to which theory has academic persuasion, I shall leave this to the judgment of my readers.

Not long after the end of the war, in 1948, I was chairman of a symposium entitled "The Sources of the Culture of the Japanese People and the Formation of the Japanese State." A report of this symposium was published in the issue of *Minzoku-gaku kenkyū* [Studies in ethnology] that appeared in the following year, and it aroused a great academic controversy as the "equestrian people theory." Although unfortunately I have not met any countertheories which have upset this theory, the general reaction seems to have been negative. The report was later published in book form under the title *Nihon minzoku no kigen* [The origins of the Japanese people]. Furthermore, last year at the Research Institute for Japanese Culture of Tōhoku University, once again Namio Egami,[6] Mitsusada Inoue,[7] Yukio Kobayashi, Nobuo Ito,[8] Akira Seki,[9] and I held a symposium on the origins of the Japanese state. Recently a report of this symposium has been published under the title *Nihon kokka no kigen* [The origins of the Japanese state].

In this volume, Egami's equestrian people theory is developed in more detail and includes responses to various criticisms he had received since the previous symposium was held.[10] Egami has in addition published his recent views in a very comprehensive monograph entitled "Nihon ni okeru minzoku no keisei to kokka no kigen" [The formation of the people in Japan and the origins of the state], which appeared in the 1967 issue of *Proceedings of the Tōyō Bunka Kenkyūsho*.

Now I shall set forth in five or six categories the bases for Egami's conclusion that only the equestrian people theory offers justification for certain interpretations.

The Bases of the Equestrian People Theory

According to the accepted views of historians,

6. 1906—. An archaeologist who specializes in the ancient history of East Asia.

7. 1917—. A historian, Inoue has made comprehensive studies of ancient Japanese history based on recent scholarship in the fields of archaeology, cultural anthropology, and philology.

8. 1908—. An archaeologist who has conducted research on the Tomb Age.

9. 1919—. A historian whose special field of interest has been the immigrants from Korea who brought important cultural skills to Japan during the fifth and sixth centuries.

10. Briefly outlined, the theory is as follows. During the fourth to the fifth centuries in the Far East, waves of northern nomadic horse-riding peoples invaded regions to the south, settled in agricultural lands, and founded states over which they ruled. In north China, they established the Sixteen Kingdoms, and in Korea the kingdom of Koguryo. There is a strong possibility that the Paekche dynasty was not Korean but Tungusic Puyo. There are also grounds for thinking that a branch of these peoples crossed the seas, conquered the people of Wa, and became the ruling elite in Japan.

Egami bases the above hypothesis on the fact that there was a Yayoi culture common to southern Korea and northern Kyūshū; that King Chin, ruler of Ma-han, Pyon-han, and Chin-han in southern Korea, appeared to be a conqueror from the north; that in Korea the era of the Three Kingdoms shows characteristics of a northern culture while similarly a marked change can be seen in the funerary objects of tombs of this time in Japan (the middle Tomb Age exhibits a strong continental influence); and finally that the emperor Sujin's name could be interpreted as meaning "ruler of Mimana," and it was this emperor whom Egami saw as the center of a movement from southern Korea to northern Kyūshū at about the beginning of the fourth century. He was the forerunner of the emperors Ōjin and Nintoku. The people of Wa had already embarked on unifying the country with Yamato as the center of power. The new equestrian people established their rule in that region by the end of the fourth century or the beginning of the fifth century. When Mimana was oppressed from the north, they sent armies to Mimana to restore their power. The period of stability that followed was the period under Ōjin's dynasty when many immigrants came over to Japan from Korea. Egami interprets this movement as the result of the ruling elite's use of these kinsmen to strengthen their control of conquered territories in Japan.

Egami's theory has been criticized by scholars of Asian history, archaeologists, and philologists. His assumption, based on a Chinese literary source, the *Giryaku* [*Wei-lüeh*, in Chinese], that King Chin was a conqueror has been questioned. Also, archaeologists have maintained that the changes in funerary objects were "evolutionary," not "revolutionary." They have also pointed out that there was no evidence of equestrian customs in Japan before Ōjin and Nintoku, which made it doubtful that the preceding emperor, Sujin, had been a conqueror. In addition, the Japanese chronicles did not indicate that Sujin was a conqueror from overseas.

However, Mitsusada Inoue points out that there are cultural elements in customs and language in ancient Japan that are distinctly north Asian as well as Southeast Asian. The Egami theory offers

it was in the fourth and fifth centuries that the Japanese people accomplished the unification of their state. Nothing has appeared yet among the relics of the burial mounds to show that the Yamato court, immediately after achieving a unified state in the fourth century, adopted continental-style cavalry as an institution. However, according to the well-known memorial inscription of King Hot'ae[11] of Koguryo, a Korean record, the people of Wa of that period, like the later Wa pirates, engaged in rather large-scale military actions in the Korean peninsula. Probably it cannot be confirmed from the memorial of King Hot'ae alone that these activities were on a large scale, but in the *Nihon-shoki* there is a narrative of a Korean invasion undertaken by the empress Jingū[12] which records that the Yamato court embarked on a conquest of Korea and engaged in military action in the Korean peninsula, after which a great number of Koreans who later became naturalized came over to Japan. This chronicle was not compiled until the early eighth century at the Yamato court, so there is room for considerable doubt as to the nature of the military action described and whether or not this was an actual event. However, there is, at any rate, this memorial inscription in northern Korea dating from about the end of the fourth century. If this could be shown to be the record of a military action undertaken by the Wa, it would mean that the action took place at about the end of the fourth century. If this, in turn, could be shown to have been a military campaign undertaken by the Yamato court, we could say with confidence that the institution of cavalry influenced by the customs of the "barbarians" already existed in the Korean peninsula at that time.

It seems doubtful, based on our general knowledge of world history, that the Japanese, who did not possess cavalry, could have invaded Korea and engaged in a campaign of conquest with only armed foot soldiers in a country where cavalry was already established and where, in contrast to Japan, the superior martial arts of China or the arms of the northern equestrian peoples were already known.

Even the military might of the great Han Empire had been repeatedly challenged by the northern equestrian peoples. In the Chinese chronicles it is recorded that the founder of the Han dynasty, finding himself surrounded by a great army of the Hsiung-nu, fled for his life from the fortified town of Pai-ti. In the preceding Warring States period, at about the end of the fourth century, the equestrian peoples were active and rode on horseback shooting arrows with strong bows in military engagements known as the "northern barbarian cavalry expeditions." In contrast to this, there are documents which record that until the end of the fourth century there was no institution of cavalry in China. In China at that time, cavalry did not exist, and a charioteer with an archer drove a two-wheeled military vehicle, like the "chariot" of Greece and Rome, drawn by two or four horses at full speed. Such were the chariots that confronted the large troops of cavalry. The cavalry could adapt itself flexibly to any kind of terrain, whereas the chariots could act effectively in engagements on a plain but in hilly country were soon overcome.

Therefore, the famous King Wu-ling of Chao, at the end of the fourth century before Christ, abandoned the old customs of middle China and said, "I wish to wear the costume of the Hu and ride on horseback, and teach my people to do likewise." In other words, even if the crowds laughed at him, in order to defend the Chinese territory to the utmost, he would adopt the military skills of the Hu. Their costume consisted of a jacket and trousers suitable for horseback riding, from which the present-day Western suit and Chinese costume are derived. The king thus

one clue to the paradox in Japanese culture of an agricultural people with a southern rice-growing culture whose speech is of northern Ural-Altaic lineage. Japanese mythology also reveals both southern and northern characteristics.

11. Reigned 391–412. A king of Koguryo in ancient Korea who led successful campaigns against the south, including territory held by the Japanese.

12. The Japanese chronicles narrate the events of the time of Empress Jingū (sometimes spelled Jingō), who was regent from A.D. 200 to 269. The legend about her conquest of Korea may reflect a historical fact of later times (the empress Sainei's journey to Kyūshū to rescue Paekche, which took place in the middle of the seventh century) or it may have some religious significance. Among those who support the latter interpretation are Kunio Yanagita and Mitsusada Inoue. The empress is said to have become a medium or shamanic diviner, god-possessed at the beginning of the expedition. Three sea gods were revealed by name in her shaman-like rite, the expedition to Silla was successful, and upon her return the empress gave birth to a prince, who later became the emperor Ōjin.

Inoue explains that the Japanese chroniclers identified Jingū with Queen Himiko of the *Wei chih* records and therefore gave Jingū legendary dates in the third century. The Korean records and King Hot'ae's memorial inscription describe Japanese military actions in Korea during the latter half of the fourth century. Japanese power in southern Korea came to an end in 562. Until then the Japanese control of Mimana and the arrival of skilled Korean immigrants brought significant continental influences to Japanese culture.

declared he would wear this costume, ride on a horse, institute cavalry, and fight. This record of King Wu-ling of Chao adopting the institution of equestrian archery in the face of opposition is extremely interesting, and is referred to in Ssu-ma Ch'ien's *Shih chi*[13] and in the *Chan kuo ts'e*.[14] It seems that it was difficult for even the Chinese troops of the Spring and Autumn period[15] and the Warring States period[16] to stand up against the military strategy of the cavalry.

In view of this, would it have been possible for a backward people who had barely accomplished unification and who lacked cavalry to cross the sea and invade and conquer a country possessing a developed cavalry? This certainly constitutes a major question.

There are other problems, too. Later in history, the Japanese Yamato court lost its bases in the Korean peninsula one by one and finally abandoned Korea. In spite of this, it is recorded that the Yamato court made persistent claims to the Chinese court listing the names of kingdoms in the Korean peninsula which had already been lost and no longer existed, and demanding recognition of Japanese sovereignty over these kingdoms.

In this period, the king of Paekche, one of the Three Kingdoms,[17] was already paying tribute to China, even before the king of Wa had begun to do so, and he received the title "King of Paekche, East-Subduing General" from the state of South Sung.[18] Now, the king of Wa protested to China that Paekche should be under the sovereignty of Wa. It is a historical fact that the Yamato court strongly demanded recognition by China of the titles "King of Wa-koku, East-Subduing General, Governor of the Six States of Wa, Paekche, Koguryo, Imna, Chin-han, and Mok-han."[19] Interpretation of this is a mystery, the solution of which is surely the task of historians. It would be inadequate to argue that Wa, a country bumpkin

13. "Records of the historian," a history of China and of all regions and peoples known at that time, which became a model for subsequent Chinese dynastic histories.

14. "Documents or intrigues of the Warring States," written during the Former Han period (202 B.C.–A.D. 9); one of the sources used by Ssu-ma Ch'ien for his *Shih chi*.

15. 722–481 B.C. A period characterized by warfare and diplomacy among the many states in north China, and the Sinicization of the south. Confucius (c. 551–479 B.C.) lived and taught during this period.

16. 403–221 B.C. A period in which there was warfare among the seven major states in China, ending with the unification of China by the state of Ch'in in 221 B.C.

17. The other two were Koguryo and Silla. The Three Kingdoms period (313–660) ended in the dominance of Silla after 660.

18. 420–479. One of the Six Dynasties in the south of China.

19. In Japanese, the last three are Mimana (territory in Korea conquered by Japan), Shinkan, and Bakan. These three states were in the south of Korea. The king of Wa was claiming authority over military affairs in Japan and the greater part of Korea, according to an "Account of the Eastern and Southern Barbarians" in the *Liu Sung shu* [History of the Liu Sung dynasty], compiled about 513. Mimana was eventually absorbed by Silla in 562.

in the distant east far from China, was ignorant of world trends and merely bragging. Alternatively, we might hypothesize that this claim of sovereignty, listing the proper names of specific places, might have been based on some reality in the past.

Myths concerning the Foundation of Japan and Korea

The third intriguing question concerns the fact that in the Japanese foundation myths of the *Kojiki* and *Nihon-shoki*, especially in the myth of the descent of the divine descendant, there are passages and place names identical with those in the foundation myths of ancient Korea.

I take the scholar's point of view that myths reflect some historical reality of the past. In other words, if there seems to be a connection between myth and historical reality, the scientific attitude should be to try to identify and substantiate this connection.

Now, the fact that there are so many points of similarity—even identity—between the foundation myths of Japan and Korea raises questions. There are many similar motifs in the myths of these two countries. For instance, the element in the Japanese stories of a child born through the influence of sunlight, without a father, becoming the founder of the ruling dynasty can also be discovered in the Korean stories. There is also the traditional motif of the foundation myths of the Three Kingdoms of Korea and of other countries in which a god descends directly from heaven and builds a country in a certain land. Scholars have often pointed out, for example, how in the foundation legends of Kara-koku,[20] that is, Mimana or Imna, there is not only an identity of form with the Japanese myth of the descent of the heavenly decendant, but also the place names "Kushi" and "Furu" appear many

20. Karak, in Korean.

times. These place names are found in the Japanese foundation myth as Kushi-furu-no-take, and Hiuga no Takachiho-no-mine Kushi-furu. "Furu" in Korean signifies a village, and "Kushi" is identical with the "Kushi" place name found in the chronicle of Kara-koku referred to above. In the *Nihon-shoki*, this "Kushi furu" is written with characters that can be pronounced "sohori," and since the capital of Paekche was "Sohoru," and the present capital of the Republic of Korea is Seoul, we may conclude that these are all Korean terms signifying the capital, or residence of the king.

Again, both Korean and Japanese legends tell us of the first ruler descending from the skies to rule the land upon receiving the heavenly decree from the deity, as set forth in the *Kojiki*: "This land has been entrusted to you as the land you are to rule. In accordance with the command, descend from the heavens!"[21] Furthermore, in the *Kojiki* and *Nihon-shoki* it is recorded that the heavenly grandson softly descended to the earth wrapped in a "matoko-o-ou-fusuma," which was a sort of cloth also called *futon* or *fusuma*, and the Kara-koku foundation legends also tell of someone descending to earth wrapped in a kind of red cloth. Thus, the motif of a descent by someone wrapped in cloth is common to both. As Namio Egami points out in his theory, this too shows affinity with the customs followed in the northern countries on the accession of a new ruler.

These strong similarities between place names and motifs in the Japanese and Korean foundation myths cannot be mere coincidence. How, then, can one explain their existence? If the Yamato court unified the country solely within the Japanese islands, without any connection to the Korean peninsula, how can we explain the similarities that survive fragmentarily in the later chronicles? Are they merely coincidental? This question too needs to be resolved.

21. *Kojiki*, trans. Donald L. Philippi (Tokyo: University of Tokyo Press, 1968), pp. 137–38. The Sun Goddess, Amaterasu, sent her grandson, Prince Ninigi, to rule the "Luxuriant reed-plain land of fresh rice-ears," namely, Japan. She bestowed upon him the sacred jewels, the mirror, and the divine sword, which became the imperial regalia. The charisma of the imperial office was thus a gift of the Sun Goddess, who was herself a shamanic diviner. The heavenly descent is an ancient myth of North Asiatic origin, possibly Tungusic, which, whether Korean or Japanese, contains the common elements of a deity or ruler's descent from heaven to a mountaintop, a divine mandate, and certain sacred regalia.

The Rivalry of Two Powers and the Entry of the Kika-jin[22]

The fourth problem concerns the fact that in the Japanese myths there are, throughout the process of unification by the Yamato court, two rival powers. This has been pointed out by various scholars since the Meiji era, and it indicates the rivalry between the two powers, the dynasty of the Yamato line (the *amatsu-kami*) and the Izumo dynasty (the *kunitsu-kami*).[23] However, there do not seem to have been any bloody conflicts between the two. As if it were the leitmotif of Japanese mythology, everywhere appears the theme of how the great power of "Ōkuni-nushi-no-mikoto"[24] of Izumo, who first ruled the land, yielded the land to the power of the Heavenly Descendant, that is, through the cession of authority by means of political compromise, unification was accomplished by the Yamato court. Furthermore, these two powers appear in the structure of the mythology to have kinship ties; for instance, in the narrative, Susano-o-no-mikoto is the brother of Amaterasu-ō-mikami, and the son or grandson of Susano-o-no-mikoto is the Ōkuni-nushi-no-mikoto of Izumo. However, the myths of the *Kojiki* and *Nihon-shoki* lead to the interpretation that originally the Izumo dynasty ruled the Japanese islands, and that the power of the Heavenly Descendants from the Heavenly Plains arrived later and through political compromise with the native Izumo power achieved unification.

In addition, there are scattered but frequent references to both powers traveling to and from, or having close relations with, the Korean peninsula. One example from the *Nihon-shoki* records that "at this time, Susano-o-no-mikoto, accompanied by his son Isotakeru-no-kami, descended to the

22. See below, n. 28.

23. Literally, heavenly gods and earthly gods. The relations between the Yamato rulers and the rulers of the Izumo region on the northern shore of the main island, who recognized the sovereignty of the former, are narrated in the *Kojiki,* the *Nihon-shoki*, and the *Izumo fudoki* (one of the very few surviving reports of a series of geographical surveys of the provinces compiled for the central government by local officials in the eighth century).

In the cycle of legends which has its setting in Izumo, the two heroes are the quarrelsome brother of the Sun Goddess, Susano-o, and his descendant, Ōkuni-nushi. Susano-o is banished from the High Heavenly Plain because of his misdeeds and goes to the province of Izumo, where he kills an eight-headed dragon and rescues a princess, whom he marries. The iron sword he discovers in the dragon's tail is symbolic of an iron-producing district in Izumo. Scholars have suggested that the dragon was the Hino River in that province, and that Susano-o may have been a local leader who tamed the floods of this river and its tributaries with dikes. (The English scholars W. G. Aston and E. Hartland have pointed out the resemblance of this legend to the Greek legend of Perseus and Andromeda.)

Before the descent of her grandson to rule Japan, the Sun Goddess took counsel with the heavenly gods, since the *kunitsu-kami* were unruly. Messengers were sent until finally Ōkuni-nushi agreed to resign (when a promise was made to build a shrine to worship him; this, it is said, is the origin of the Great Shrine of Izumo, which is second only to the shrine of the Sun Goddess at Ise). The land-cession legend reflects the power of the rival Izumo rulers and their surrender to the sovereignty of the Yamato line not through conquest but through an agreement which recognized their spiritual authority. Izumo appears either to be representative of Japan or to be the last region that the Yamato rulers subdued.

24. Ōkuni-nushi means "The Master of the Great Land." "Mikoto" and "Kami" are titles used for the deities. Ōkuni-nushi, the most famous hero of Japanese mythology, has been interpreted as the personification of the Izumo rulers and their exploits. Izumo was not a province of rich material resources, and it is possible that its prestige arose from its relations with Korea.

Ōkuni-nushi had many older brothers who courted a certain princess. They ordered Ōkuni-nushi to accompany them and carry their bags. Along the way, they saw a naked rabbit which had been skinned by a crocodile, and they told him to bathe in salt water and lie on a mountain peak where the wind would blow on him. Ōkuni-nushi came along last and took pity on the rabbit, crying in pain after having done as the brothers instructed him. Ōkuni-nushi told the rabbit to wash off the salt and roll on the pollen of the *gama* grass, which would heal him. The rabbit was accordingly healed and told Ō-kuni-nushi that he would gain the princess. This is a favorite children's story even today. Interpreting it, modern scholars have associated Ōkuni-nushi with shamanistic practices of magic healing.

Subsequently the brothers of Ōkuni-nushi became jealous and put him through ordeals which caused him to die, but each time he was miraculously restored to life. Some scholars have seen in this legend a resemblance to the initiation rites of primitive tribes, and it may reflect the trials that

land of Silla, where he dwelt at Soshimori," and "There he lifted up his voice and said:—'I will not dwell in this land.' He at length took clay and made of it a boat, in which he embarked, and crossed over eastwards until he arrived at Mount [Torigamine], which is by the upper waters of the river Hi in Izumo."[25] This passage describes travel to and from the Korean peninsula, that is, going to Kara-kuni in Korea and returning to Izumo. Again, there is a passage in the *Kojiki* on the descent of Ninigi-no-mikoto upon Mount Takachiho of Hiuga in Tsukushi:[26] "At this time he said: 'This place is opposite the land of Kara; (it is a place to which one) comes directly through the Cape of Kasasa, a land where the morning sun shines directly, a land where the rays of the evening sun are brilliant. This is a most excellent place.' "[27] Thus the relation with the Korean peninsula is constantly reiterated.

Of course, there are many other persons appearing in the Japanese mythology in connection with Korea. In any case, the theme of rivalry and compromise between two powers and the records of the close relations with the Korean peninsula form one of the characteristics of the *Kojiki* and the *Nihon-shoki*. If the eighth-century court had created the Japanese mythology purely for political purposes, there would have been no need for them to elaborate such themes. It must be concluded that it was impossible to compile the *Kojiki* and *Nihon-shoki* without taking into account the old legends or material already chronicled in various records.

The fifth question concerns the fact that, after the establishment of the rule of the Yamato court, aliens with new skills, who later became naturalized, migrated to Japan in great numbers from the Korean peninsula or the continent, coming mainly through the peninsula, and were highly favored by the court.[28] Many scholars have pointed out that, in the regions where they lived in Japan, they have left vestiges of their old homes in place names or in their family line. According to the Japanese records of the fourth and fifth centuries, a great many immigrants came during the reigns of Ōjin and Nintoku. This immigration continued for a long time afterward. Detailed research by historians has made clear that the greatest wave of immigration took place immediately after the unification of Japan by the Yamato court. If the Yamato court was established without any relation to Korea, how can these facts be explained? Surely if relations between Japan and Korea had been distant or nonexistent in the past, such an influx would not have taken place, bringing with it such close relations.

I have now raised five questions. If we were to view them as isolated problems solely within the framework of Japanese history, it might be possible to work out some kind of explanation for each one of them. However, if we consider these questions together, within the context of contemporary Asian history, the possibility of finding a valid interpretation based upon events occurring among the Wa people in isolation from the continent is extremely slim.

In effect, Egami's equestrian people theory is an approach to the study of the Japanese state within the mainstream of contemporary Asian history or world history, rather than an attempt to solve these questions within the narrower framework of Japanese history. It is, I think, a hypothesis that points the way to a clear interpretation of the five questions I raised and the great qualitative changes seen in the early to middle periods of the Tomb Age.

preceded the success of Ōkuni-nushi in becoming the ruler of Izumo. In the legend, he finally pursues and subdues his brothers.

25. *Nihongi: Chronicles of Japan from the Earliest Times to A.D. 697*, trans. W. G. Aston (London: George Allen and Unwin, 1956), p. 57.

26. The ancient name for Kyūshū.

27. *Kojiki*, trans. Donald L. Philippi (Tokyo: University of Tokyo Press, 1968), p. 141.

28. The Chinese and Korean immigrants who came to Japan in fluctuating waves mainly from about 200 B.C. to the latter half of the seventh century were responsible for the introduction of the superior cultural elements of continental civilization, including knowledge of Buddhism, Chinese writing, and the fine arts. The term *kika-jin* or *torai-jin* is generally associated with the Korean refugees who began to cross over to Japan about A.D. 400 to escape the disturbances caused by dynastic upheavals, and who continued to arrive during the fifth and sixth centuries.

The Validity of the Equestrian People Theory

Egami based his theory of the equestrian people on Teikichi Kita's[29] theories, published under the title *Nissen dōgen ron* [A study of the common origins of Japan and Korea] in the Taishō era. To summarize Kita's conclusions, the founding of the Japanese state has a continuous relationship both temporally and geographically with the founding of the Three Kingdoms in Korea, Paekche, Silla, and Koguryo, after the early migrations of the Tungusic Puyo and Koguryo from the north, and should be considered within the context of Asian history. Also, the processes of the founding of these two states closely resemble one another. Might not the nucleus of government have been one of the northeast Asia equestrian peoples which, during this turbulent era on the Chinese continent, moved southward into the Korean peninsula? Since the Yayoi Age, the Wa people and the people of Kan, ancient Korea, had been looked upon as distinct and separate with regard to language and other factors, but their relationship then was closer than in later times, and they may well have formed a single cultural sphere extending on both sides of the Tsushima Straits. I too tentatively favor this approach. I think it may be surmised that the equestrian people held sway over a broad area, perhaps a federation of the Wa and Kan stretching over southern Korea and western Japan. This regime had its base in southern Korea rather than in Japan and ruled over the peoples of both Wa and Kan. Due to the formation and development of other states in the Korean peninsula, this power was eventually shut out of the peninsula and finally ruled only in Japan. During this time, it presumably transferred the center of its influence to the territory of the Wa people in the Japanese islands, where no strong political

29. 1871–1939. A scholar of Japanese history, with a special interest in ancient history based on archaeological and folklore sources. From 1916 onward, Kita (sometimes spelled "Kida") published a series of studies on the people of Wa. He was known for his original approach to ancient history, and for having been dismissed from the Tokyo Imperial University (now the University of Tokyo) in 1911, because he gave equal weight to the rival imperial courts of the Northern and Southern Dynasties (1336–92) in a textbook written for schoolteachers. The southern court returned to Kyoto in 1392 after a reconciliation, but the Southern Dynasty was excluded from the throne thereafter. Kita's expulsion is an instance of the political pressure put upon scholars to conform to the policy of exaltation of the "imperial rule." In 1921, Kita published a study based on sources from archaeology, ethnology, etymology, and history which stressed the common origins of Japan and Korea and extended to the ties between the Japanese and the peoples of Manchuria and Mongolia. In contrast to this approach, some historians of the recent postwar period have tried to study the unique features of Korean history, rather than emphasizing the foreign influences upon Korean civilization.

authority existed. Thus, from about the fourth to the fifth century, a great political center was established in Yamato, but it is conceivable that at that time the rulers retained some power extending into the Korean peninsula.

However, in later chronicles these events were completely ignored, and the retreat from the Korean peninsula was assumed to have taken place after the reign of Emperor Tenji.[30] Furthermore, the concepts of the founding of Japan also began to change greatly. And in the Nara period the court began, for political purposes, to claim that the reigning family was a traditional dynasty founded in the timeless past. At the beginning of the eighth century the *Kojiki* and *Nihon-shoki* were compiled with this political aim in view. In this respect, Egami's ideas come close to those of Sōkichi Tsuda, but in regard to the interpretation of the mythology that preceded the writing of these chronicles they differ greatly from the latter's theory and fully explore the points raised by Teikichi Kita.

If we follow the hypothesis known as the equestrian people theory, the five questions just raised and the cultural gap between the early and middle periods of the Tomb Age can be fairly clearly explained. In effect, we can understand the reason the king of Wa, who had ruled for the most part in the Korean peninsula, still made emphatic claims to China concerning the legitimacy of his sovereignty in southern Korea, even after he had moved to the Japanese islands. Egami contends that it is very easy to understand the contacts with the Korean peninsula since the "theocratic age," or the great immigration following the reign of Emperor Ōjin, when these are seen in relation to the Yamato dynasty's conquest and founding of the country.

This is similar to what happened after the Mongolians of the great Yuan Empire[31] chose

30. Emperor of Japan, 662–671.

31. 1260–1368. The rise of the nomadic Mongols was spectacular. Their prowess as horsemen and archers under the leadership of Genghis Khan led to conquests culminating two generations later in the conquest of South Sung by Kublai Khan in 1260. They maintained their large empire by a transportation system described by Marco Polo and relied upon Chinese and Sinicized non-Chinese for counsel in government.

Peking as their capital, when the so-called *shiki-moku* people[32] from the western borderlands belonging to the Turkish or Iranian races, referred to since the T'ang era[33] as "purple-bearded green-eyed" people, were invited in great numbers by the Yuan court, bringing with them new technical skills from the west and later becoming naturalized in China. Their descendants are Chinese-speaking Muslims who remain in China today. In other words, they retain certain cultural traits of their forefathers.

Consequently, in order to refute Egami's theory one must refute in entirety the five points which constitute the bases of his reasoning, together with the sixth point, namely, the archaeological gap. These are interrelated questions, so to counter one or two points alone would not constitute a satisfactory refutation of the theory. Criticism of the equestrian people theory should arise, I think, from a synthesis of all the different disciplines based on a broad historical perspective.

Unfortunately, there has been no synthetic criticism offered by those who reject the equestrian people theory. Recently, however, historians holding moderate views have maintained that those elements that can be confirmed should be acknowledged. For instance, in Mitsusada Inoue's *Shinwa yori rekishi e* [From mythology to history], volume 1 of *Nihon no rekishi* [The history of Japan], and his *Kodai kokka no kenkyū* [A study of the ancient state in Japan], the author has not taken an entirely negative attitude toward the theory. As detailed and meticulous documentary analysis accumulates, the regime of Ōjin, which was undoubtedly historical, appears to have been a strong conquering force in its expansion from Kyūshū to Yamato. This interpretation is also maintained in Inoue's *Nihon kokka no kigen* [The origins of the Japanese state].

32. These people included the Uighur and Tangut tribes.

33. 618–906. One of the most brilliant periods in Chinese history, during which the cultural influence of China had a profound effect upon Korea and Japan. In Nara and Kyoto, the Japanese copied the plan of Ch'ang-an, the Chinese capital, and relied heavily on the inspiration of Chinese art, literature, religion, and administrative organization. International trade and a cosmopolitan atmosphere drew Japanese statesmen, scholars, students, artists, and businessmen to Changan. The Nara period (710–794) was thus comparable to the Meiji period (1868–1912), when Japan was also nuder a strong foreign influence. Some of the political and social reforms carried out in imitation of Chinese institutions proved unsuitable, but other achievements were enduring. The Japanese learned more advanced methods in sericulture, textile manufacturing, paper making, woodworking, and printing. Buddhism and Buddhist art were patronized by the emperor Shōmu (724–749). Confucianism also contributed to changes in moral values. Chinese music, dancing, and other arts (sculpture in wood, bronze, clay, and lacquer, painting, and architecture) were appreciated, and Japanese artists have left masterpieces which reveal a Chinese style but already possess a Japanese quality.

Unification and Formation of the People

At this point, I must offer a final word of caution. The unification of the state by the Yamato court is an undoubted historical fact. Its power was established first in western Japan; then, eventually, the Japanese islands from Kyūshū to the northeast were bound together in a single unified state. This fact must have provided a kind of framework for the Japanese language, or the consolidation of Japanese culture, and given the Japanese a racial bond formed through group consciousness. I made it clear at the beginning that a state and a people are two separate concepts, but in world history there are numerous examples of how the political framework of a state greatly influences the formation of a people. Yet there are also cases in which it has proved impossible to consolidate a people, however strong the framework of the state might be. When Japan annexed Korea in 1910, even the use of the Korean language was prohibited, but of course such a foolish policy could not succeed. Such instances can be found anywhere. On the other hand, are we not witnessing the process by which the framework of a consolidated state, the United States of America, is actually forming a single new people, the American people? In any case, we must recognize that the unification of the state by the Yamato court is inextricably linked with the formation of the Japanese people.

Again, many scholars think that the Japanese language is close to the Altaic languages, but, granted this, it is unlikely that the language of the post-Nara period had its roots in the speech of the new ruling class, which centered around the imperial family initially at the time of the formation of the Yamato court. As mentioned before, it is quite certain that the language of the Wa people since the Yayoi Age has been, essentially, the Japanese of today. If this language was Altaic, it seems safe to assume that the people of the Yayoi Age also spoke an Altaic language.

What relation is there, then, between the Japanese language of today and this process of the formation of a state through conquest? Even if the founders of the Yamato state were an alien conquering people, they were probably, as could be seen everywhere in contemporary Asian history, a relatively small mobile military force consisting largely of men. Even though politically they completely overwhelmed and controlled the kingdom of the Wa people, as also happened when conquering dynasties overcame the Han people, from the linguistic and cultural point of view it was rather the conquerors who were assimilated and absorbed by the people they ruled. Indeed, because of such a process, the *Kojiki* and the *Nihon-shoki*, compiled in the eighth century, while everywhere retaining records of a conquering dynasty, yet maintain that the original legitimate sovereignty of the Japanese land was based on a mission given by Heavenly Deities. We may tentatively interpret this as the structuring of Japanese history in the eighth century to show that the country had been created from the beginning in the Japanese islands, and that from around the reign of Ōjin a great movement of conquest had been initiated toward the Korean peninsula.

In any case, regardless of the justification for the equestrian people theory, my own theories on the formation of Japanese culture have not changed. A primitive version of the Japanese culture was formed in the Yayoi Age, based on rice growing. Whether we assume that the Yamato court arose from among the Wa powers alone and unified the country, or from a military force somewhat alien to the people of Wa—probably a northern people whose language may have been Altaic but was nonetheless rather different from the speech of the Wa people—in the final analysis we may conclude that the Japanese people were rooted in the cultural and linguistic tradition of the Wa people, who had maintained a rice-based culture since the Yayoi Age. This culture could not be fundamentally overthrown by political conquest or unification. Egami too, I believe, supports this line of reasoning.

The Reception of Foreign Civilization and the Sources of Culture

Frequently the equestrian people theory has been misunderstood, and people have described the Japanese language itself as having been introduced by a conquering equestrian people speaking an Altaic language, which became the basis for the present-day Japanese language; but the evidence does not justify this view. Of course, Egami himself seems to believe that there are other possibilities in addition to those raised by Ohno with regard to the lineage of the Japanese language. However, the question of the Altaic linguistic structure may be explained, I believe, as I have done.

It is a well-known fact that Japanese culture developed under the influence of the Asian continent, as various elements of Chinese culture, including Buddhism,[34] were enthusiastically imported by the Yamato court. However, I do not agree that the sources of Japanese culture can be found in the civilization that entered Japan after the unification of the state. This approach would have something in common with the view that the origins of the culture of the German peoples can be found in Christianity, or that the sources of present-day Western European civilization may be sought in the civilizations of Greece and Rome, but this kind of explanation is not always justifiable.

Just as Christianity or the civilizations of Greece and Rome are inextricably related to present-day Western European civilization, Japanese culture is

34. Buddhism was introduced into Japan about 550 or perhaps a decade earlier, with gifts of images and scriptures from Paekche, which needed aid from Japan against its enemies, Silla and Koguryo. The results were far-reaching, and Buddhism was influential in establishing a higher morality in Japan. Yet in its later development, Buddhism was transformed by Japanese tradition and became a Japanese religion. Confucianism developed in Japan not as a separate religion but as a political and social philosophy which was accepted when Chinese models of government were followed. The Confucian idea of social harmony was valued in Japan: the ideal of a just ruler and a people loyal to the ruler, that is, the emperor, looked upon as the Son of Heaven, according to the Chinese idea of Heaven ordaining the ruler. The Confucian emphasis upon filial piety also appealed to the Japanese, who had a tradition of revering the dead. Shintoism, the native religious tradition, cooperated with Buddhism, and the Kami or Shinto gods became identified with Buddhas and bodhisattvas. Buddhism gave Shintoism a philosophy as well as ritual and architectural forms.

closely connected with Buddhism and the superior civilization of the Han people of the Chinese continent. However, it would not be correct to say that no unique Japanese culture existed before the influx of foreign elements. The German peoples also possessed their own native culture, of an ancient Indo-European linguistic heritage, before the transmission to Northern Europe of the civilizations of Greece and Rome in the pre-Christian era. The racial character, or what the Germans call *Germānentūm*, which the northern European peoples have maintained continuously to the present day, had already established its identity before Christianity or the civilizations of Greece and Rome were introduced, and its tradition lives on today as one of the bases of their culture.

In the case of the Japanese people, too, it is unlikely that the Japanese culture was first formed upon the basis of the influx of Buddhism or of continental civilization. These are the forces that shaped and nurtured the culture of the Japanese people, and therefore we cannot ignore the influence of continental civilization in a study of Japanese culture, but before they were molded by foreign culture the Japanese already possessed a distinct character of their own. This unique character, which will not easily change as long as the Japanese survive as a people, must have evolved from the life of the rice-growing people of the Yayoi Age before the unification of the state or the introduction of continental civilization.

Long ago, Motoori Norinaga[35] used the phrase *Yamato gokoro* in contrast to the phrase *Karagokoro no sakashira*,[36] and so claimed a distinctive way of life for the "pure" Japanese, in other words, the existence of a racial individuality. Norinaga sought this in the world of the *Kojiki* and tried to clarify its nature. Using the academic language of today, I would suggest that the traditions of the rice-growing farm communities maintained since the

35. 1730–1801. Author of a commentary on the *Kojiki* which took him thirty-five years to complete, and which remains a classic in Japanese literature. Motoori Norinaga was the greatest leader of the *kokugaku* (national learning) movement of the seventeenth and eighteenth centuries. Shintoism had rarely been expressed in systematic terms and had tended to borrow from both Buddhism and Confucianism. *Kokugaku* was a reaction against this religious syncretism and an attempt to clarify the basic value system of Japan. This field of scholarship was "connected with the Japanese search for cultural identity or a national self-image" (Shigeru Matsumoto, *Motoori Norinaga: 1730–1801* [Cambridge: Harvard University Press, 1970], p. 1).

36. *Yamato gokoro*, or the Japanese spirit, was the essence of the Ancient Way or the "Way of the *kami*," recorded in the *Kojiki* and to a lesser degree in the *Nihonshoki* and other writings; the ancient practices were thought to embody truth and living reality. In contrast, *Karagokoro no sakashira*, or the Chinese spirit, meant a Sino-centric or Sino-philic attitude. *Kara* meant China; thus *Karagokoro* (literally, the spirit of China) signified reading Chinese books and falling under the influence of Chinese culture, while *sakashira* meant to feign wisdom or knowledge, so that the entire phrase might be translated as "superficial knowledge of Chinese culture." Norinaga saw in Chinese writings a concern for the rational and explanatory which overlooked the limitations of human reason and the inscrutable aspect of reality.

Yayoi Age can also be seen in various ways in the world of the *Kojiki*. It is here that the basic character of the Japanese culture untouched by the influence of the advanced continental culture can be found.

Then again, in discussions today on the national character of the Japanese, the generally accepted view is to seek its prototype in the "personality" of the farmer. Our previous discussions show that there is ample reason for this. With the above viewpoint in mind, I want to discuss in the next two chapters the characteristics of Japanese culture, and the character of the Japanese which has continued to the present day.

Surely we can discover the characteristics of the Japanese, shaped by the above process, by comparing them with the peoples of the Asian continent or with the distant European peoples—using the same general technique of tracing the formation of these other peoples and their cultures back to their sources. The present characteristics of the Japanese must be connected historically with the special individuality nurtured in the infancy of the race—this is one of my hypotheses. I realize that it is impossible to support this by academic evidence here, but I cherish the dream of being able to prove this in the future.

5. The Distinctive Character of Japanese Culture

The Geographical Boundaries of Culture

Up to this point, I have concentrated mainly on studying the origins of the Japanese culture. My hypothesis is that the racial character of the Japanese and the distinctive character or "pattern" of Japanese culture are intimately related to the formation of the Japanese people. I have thought about when and how the core of the distinctive character of the Japanese was formed, and I hope to analyze, drawing on academic evidence, these questions which are parallel to the problem of the formation of the Japanese people. Needless to say, it is impossible to answer all of these questions. Consequently, the following discussion will inevitably raise further questions which will hopefully be clarified through the studies of other scholars.

The phrase Japanese culture which I use refers to the present culture of the Japanese as I originally defined it. Consequently, I will consider its distinctive character by first distinguishing it from the culture of other peoples. In order to do this, and before embarking on a comparison of Japanese culture and Western civilization, I would like to comment on the various views of the geographical boundaries that separate Japan from the rest of the world.

The first geographical boundary that exists between Japan and other countries, namely the line extending from Genkai Nada to the Tsushima Straits, poses a great problem. Of course, it is possible to consider Okinawa a single cultural sphere in itself, but we do not think of the people of Okinawa as being different from the Japanese. In fact, we recognize them as linguistically and culturally an integral part of the Japanese race. Therefore, Okinawa should be included in the Japanese archipelago, that is, what we designate as the sphere of Japanese culture. However, this boundary line of the Tsushima Straits nonetheless remains a problem.

The second problem is the division of West and East, from the Western standpoint. To the European, the entire area east of the line extending from the Mediterranean to the Bosporus is conceived of as "the East." This inevitably raises questions with regard to the division of cultural spheres in world history. From the viewpoint of the study of Japanese culture, the East as defined by the West is by no means all of one piece. In particular, the culture of the southwest Asian areas, that is, what Westerners call the Near East, and the culture of the Japanese, who are a rice-growing people of the monsoon belt of East Asia, are extremely different. This is no doubt clear from the article on the experiences of a Japanese living among the Bedouins which I discussed in Chapter 1. In fact, from the standpoint of the Japanese, the peoples of the Near East, that is, the peoples of the Islamic sphere, have a culture whose character is similar to that of the Europeans. Therefore, in contrast to the boundary drawn by Europeans looking at the East, if we look at the West from Japan and ask at what point we become conscious of the West, many Japanese would draw a boundary line between Burma and India.

A great many ideas come to me when I think of the problems involved in these three boundaries:

1. One of the Three Kingdoms (57?B.C.–A.D. 668), in the southeast of the Korean peninsula. Silla aided the Chinese of the T'ang period in destroying the other two kingdoms, Paekche in 660 and Koguryo in 668, and established a unified Korean state (668–892), which was subsequently overthrown in 935.

2. *Kara* means Chinese; *shishi* means lion. Also known as Dog of Fo, the *karashishi* is a Buddhist guardian lion, resembling a Pekinese dog, with a large bushy tail, usually found at the entrance to temples. See Margaret Medley, *A Handbook of Chinese Art* (New York: Horizon Press, 1965), pp. 66, 92.

3. Built as an auxiliary royal residence in the fourth year of the reign of King Taejong, the third Yi ruler (1404).

4. 1392–1910. The Yi dynasty developed a culture which shows marked contrast in the evolution of Buddhism and Confucianism. Buddhism flourished in the periods of the unified Silla dynasty (668–935) and the succeeding Koryo dynasty (918–1392) but acquired political and economic power during the latter period, which was the cause of a reaction under the Yi dynasty. Consequently Buddhism declined while, on the other hand, Confucian concepts of government and social relations profoundly influenced the people.

5. The Europeans were called *nambanjin* or Southern Barbarians by the Japanese in the Edo period (1603–1867), when the Tokugawa shogunate (see n. 6, below) ruled Japan from Edo, renamed Tokyo in 1868. The first Europeans came to Japan in 1543: three Portuguese whose junk was blown northeast to Tanegashima, an island south of Kyūshū. They were followed by Portuguese traders and in 1549 by the Spanish

first, the Tsushima Straits line; second, the line formed by the Bosporus Straits and the Mediterranean; and third, the north-south line dividing Burma from India.

The Tsushima Straits Line

With regard to the line of the Tsushima Straits, I would like to mention two or three visual or auditory impressions which strike the traveler, based on my own experiences during my stay in Korea last fall. One day I visited Kyongju, the capital of ancient Silla,[1] which is located, approaching it from Seoul, near the Japan Sea coast and north of Pusan. There are a great many old historic sites in the neighborhood, and toward the east of the town there is a temple called Pulguksa, a monument dating from the Silla period. There used to be a nine-storied tower, but the upper six stories fell into ruin, so now it is only a three-storied tower. At the four corners of the base of this tower are four stone effigies like the *karashishi*[2] gazing out in the four directions. They appear to have been placed there for the protection of the king's palace. They differ in shape and expression; one is glaring in the direction of Japan, while the upper half of another one is carved in the form of the kind of seal which is often found swimming southward in the Japan Sea. The Japanese would surely have known of this kind of seal which came from the northern seas, but I do not know of any Japanese sculpture in this shape. Thus, seeing it, I felt that Korean culture was indeed alien. Again, as I walked in the beautiful parks like that of the Changdok Palace[3] and looked at the palaces and sculptures of the Yi dynasty,[4] I encountered sculptures of elephants. In Japan, too, it is recorded that the Southern Barbarians[5] brought an elephant to Nagasaki in the

Tokugawa period[6] and made it walk from Nagasaki to Edo in the time of the shogun Yoshimune,[7] which created quite a sensation.

As I looked around the museums in Seoul and elsewhere, I found among the earthenware of the time corresponding to the Tomb Age in Japan a jar of a particular shape named a "flat vessel." It had a small spout and a rounded body like a slightly flattened hot water bottle. There were other variations of this shape, but these were forms rarely seen in Japan either among the old earthenware or among modern pieces. Today the people of Cheju Island still use this type of earthenware in a slightly different form, which they call *kudoku*, and both this form of earthenware and the term *kudoku* appear among the nomadic peoples of the continent. The nomads speaking Altaic languages do not use earthenware but instead make vessels for wine and milk by tanning the skins of sheep and cows. They make a spout for pouring and sew up the rest. The result is a large leather bag which is shaped like the body of an animal. Since ancient times, this kind of leather bag has been used on the northern borders of China and in the western part of Central Asia. And in the Bible we find the phrase "New wine into fresh wineskins." This kind of vessel belonged to the nomadic peoples, and the Altaic language-speaking peoples gave it names of the same lineage as *fudoku* or *kudoku*. The word *fukutoku*, indicating an earthenware piece of this type, can be found in Chinese books, and we may readily assume that this pronunciation belongs to the same lineage linguistically as the present *fudoku* of Cheju Island. In fact, research has already been done on this. Thus, we may regard this vessel as having been part of life in the Korean peninsula continuously from the Silla period to the present.

One might think that this type of vessel was not used in Japan, but this is not true. Among the Sue-style pottery[8] of the burial mounds, several of this

Jesuit missionary Saint Francis Xavier (1506–52), who remained in Japan for two years and founded many Christian communities. These Southern Barbarians left a unique heritage to Japan in religion and culture.

6. 1603–1867. The Tokugawa shogunate, established in 1603, took steps to control the trade with European countries, and, looking upon Christianity as a disruptive force, maintained a strict seclusion policy. Japan remained at peace for over two hundred years, prosperous but insular. During this period, foundations were laid for the achievement of rapid modernization after the opening of the country by Commodore Matthew Perry in 1853–54.

7. Ruled, 1716–45; d. 1757. Shogun was the title taken by the Tokugawa rulers. Minamoto-no-Yoritomo (1147–99) had been appointed *sei-i-taishōgun* (generalissimo) in 1192 and had established the *Bakufu* or shogunate at Kamakura, thus setting the pattern for a military government that lasted for seven hundred years until the fall of the Tokugawa. Shogun Yoshimune initiated economic policies which eventually failed because of weaknesses in the national economy. He encouraged learning and lifted the ban on imported books in 1720, providing they did not touch upon Christianity.

8. Typical pottery of the Tomb Age, the third to seventh centuries A.D.; grey, thin, and wheelmade.

type, called *hodoki* in Japanese, have been found. This word *hodoki* also comes from an Altaic root word, and scholarly research has revealed that the shape of this type of earthenware belongs to the lineage of the Korean *henko* and the *fukutoku* or *fudoku* of the ancient Chinese documents. However, this type of earthenware has not been used in our daily life since the Tomb Age, and it is my impression that its distribution ends at the line of the Tsushima Straits.

In the museums of the Republic of Korea there are also many vessels and earthenware pieces shaped like the horns of cattle. These too are seldom seen in Japan. Perhaps a few were made but they were rare and were not in general use. Yet, in Korea, they seem to have been used continuously as daily utensils since ancient times. Again in Korea, the Western-style horn-shaped wine cup appears to have been used. In Seoul I often saw horns carved into the shape of small flower vases for sale. This too is not a widespread custom in Japan. The wine horn can be traced back to ancient times and was widely used across the Eurasian continent, even in Europe. The word "cornucopia" means that a god has put in a horn the fruit of a harvest and holds it aloft. There are many depictions of such gods in the West. Among the more famous ones, there is a relief sculpture excavated at a site called Laussel in southern France which scholars call the paleolithic Venus, a plump nude woman holding a cow's horn in her right hand. The horn must have been linked from very ancient times with the concepts of magic and destiny. However, this cultural complex centering around the horn does not appear to have entered Japan.

The Cultural Sphere of the Key

I have also been considering the phenomenon of the use of keys. If we look at Western life, the use of keys in hotels, and indeed everywhere, is an absolute condition. When we travel in Europe and observe the old medieval houses, or look at articles in museums or in buildings dating from classical times, we find that there is a very strict system of shutting up the separate rooms by the use of keys. The development of the key is amazing, and I think this custom of locking up places with keys is a distinctive characteristic of Western civilization. Particularly in Europe, the power of the housewife is symbolized by the key. It is customary in European country weddings for the bride, dressed in the pretty costume of her province, to hang keys from her waist. Also, returning the keys signifies the abandonment of the housewife's rights. There is a clause in the twelve Roman bronze tablets about handing the keys back to the husband in case of a divorce. When the husband died, the placing of the keys on the corpse signified that the wife had given up her right to the inheritance, and it is said that this also meant the abandonment of the obligation of paying off debts. In short, the key has been widely viewed in Europe as the symbol of the housewife's rights.

Even among the Chinese, the custom of using keys was widespread. In China, too, the housewife was referred to as the person who owns the keys: *tai yau shi te* [keeper of the keys]. Although the actual keys surviving seem to be from a later date, ideographs with the signs for key and records with the word "key" in them can be seen in documents of the Chou and Han periods, so China too may be classified as belonging to the sphere of the key culture. I have not yet studied the extent of the use of keys in the life of the Korean farmer, but based on general observations I would think that, in contrast to Japan, the Korean peninsula, as part of the Chinese cultural sphere, could also be included in the key culture sphere.

What role, then, does the key play in Japanese life? Of course, we find keys as household furnishings among the Shōsō-in[9] treasures, but these were imported from China. We can also recognize the use of keys in some Japanese castles, and elsewhere. But how about the life of the ordinary townsman, and especially village life? As far as I have been able to see, the concept of using keys to lock houses and rooms seems to have been very limited. The iron key which developed in Europe was not used to any great extent in traditional daily life in Japan. Naturally, the use of keys is impractical in houses where rooms are partitioned off by screens or paper doors. These basic differences exist. In Japan, I have seen a document indicating that there are also regions where, as in Europe, the handing over of keys was used as a symbol of the housewife's rights, but almost all over the country the shakushi[10] is the equivalent of the European key in this symbolic sense. There is even a folksong in Sado that goes, "Married for six years, already with children; hand over the shakushi to this daughter-in-law."

In Hida, when the housewife's rights are passed on to the daughter-in-law, the housewife, known as kakasa,[11] who feels she is growing old and decides to spend the rest of her life in a leisurely way, on the night of the last day of the year when the family has sat down to the toshi-tori dinner,[12] seizes this occasion to say to the daughter-in-law, "Now you serve the rice to the family." This is the "handing over of the shakushi" ritual, and it is a declaration by the kakasa of the cession of her rights as housewife to the yomesa, namely, the daughter-in-law. In Japan this kind of custom is practiced, in contrast to the European custom. The boundary between the key culture sphere and the cultural sphere symbolized by screens and paper partitions may

9. A treasury on the grounds of the Buddhist temple Tōdai-ji, in Nara, which stores the relics and cultural objects from the reign of Emperor Shōmu (701–756). These objects throw light on the court life of that period and are an invaluable source for the understanding of Japan's early cultural relations with Korea and China.

10. A flat wooden spoon or paddle for serving rice.

11. Dialect for "mother," meaning the "housewife." Yomesa is the dialect term for "daughter-in-law."

12. Toshi means a year and tori, to add. Also known as toshi-koshi (koshi, pass or cross over). On New Year's Eve, the family gathers for a ritual meal, a part of the New Year celebrations. In Hida, the mountainous region of central Japan, this was made the occasion for the housewife who wished to retire from her duties to pass on her authority to her daughter-in-law, as described.

perhaps coincide with the line of the Tsushima Straits.

The Depth of Permeation of Christianity and Confucianism

Traveling through the countryside of the Republic of Korea by train, we can see in even the smallest village or town very fine church buildings with a cross above, but it is impossible to see such churches in Japanese towns and villages. Christianity seems to have permeated very deeply as far as the Korean peninsula.[13] Perhaps this reflects, in part, the Korean people's search for consolation in a worldwide religion during their colonial period under the oppressive Japanese rule. It may also reflect the fundamental and distinctive nature of their culture, namely, there may be a stronger basis there than in Japan for the reception of a religion such as Christianity. Confucianism also has entered into the life of the Korean people more deeply. The Korean sense of Confucianism is different from the Japanese. For instance, in rural areas of Korea, there is a very strict insistence upon filial piety. Judging from impressions I gathered in casual conversations with people I met, Confucian culture seems to have penetrated deeply into Korea. In Japan, too, Confucianism entered the lives of a few samurai through their education in the Chinese classics. Yet the influence of a Confucian ethic or world view is rarely seen among townsmen and is almost nonexistent among farmers.

Recently Iwanami Shoten[14] started to publish, as part of a series on the era of the great sea voyages, the records of the Spanish and the Portuguese on the East, with meticulous footnotes. The descriptions of contemporary Japan by these famous Europeans are extremely valuable to our understanding of Japanese cultural history. I myself am

13. Among the Asian nations, Christianity has been most successful in Korea. About one-twentieth of the population became Christians, in contrast to Japan, where Christians are estimated at about half a million in a population of one hundred million. It was during the period of Japanese rule (1910–45) that Christianity made progress, apparently offering religious strength and constructive activities in the fields of education and social welfare to Koreans frustrated under Japanese control. An interpretation that stresses the political implications of Christianity in Korea is expressed by Robert A. Scalapino: "For the modern Korean, Christianity became a method of expressing political as well as religious sentiments—a source of nationalist identification against Chinese and Japanese threats" ("Race Relations and United States Policy in Asia," in George W. Shepherd, Jr., ed., *Racial Influences on American Foreign Policy* [New York: Basic Books, 1970], p. 118). For the majority of Koreans, however, Confucianism provided a way of life, much as Shintoism was a way of life for the Japanese. This was actually neo-Confucianism, introduced by Korean scholars from China in the later part of the Koryo period (918–1392), or the philosophy of Chu Hsi. It provided ethical standards in family and social relationships and belief in a world controlled by a Supreme Ultimate Being. In Tokugawa Japan (1603–1867), neo-Confucianism gave a philosophical rationale to the legal and political order, but the Japanese were more pragmatic in their approach. It may be said that the Koreans are more philosophical than the Japanese.

14. A prominent Tokyo publishing company devoted to the

using them in a study of comparative culture. In particular, the reports of the contemporary Confucian-educated Korean intellectuals who came to Japan and wrote on Japanese life are extremely interesting for a comparison of our respective cultures. In their description of public baths in Japanese towns, the Koreans wrote, "Both men and women talk and laugh in the public baths without shame. They are truly beasts." Setting aside the question whether or not the contemporary Japanese were beasts, at any rate, the fact that Confucian culture had not crossed the Tsushima Straits and entered the consciousness of the common people of Japan can be amply proved. Later on, when Koreans, Chinese, or other peoples from the Asian continent came to study in Japan, there must have been a number of Japanese manners and customs they could not get used to.

There are many cases of things now extinct on the continent crossing the line of the Tsushima Straits, permeating Japan to the north, and eventually surviving only in Japan, but there are also many other things that came as far as the southern boundary of the Korean peninsula without taking the further step of crossing the straits and entering Japan. This is an extremely interesting problem.

The Eunuch Institution, Unknown in Japan

There is another similar question, namely, that of the institution of eunuchs employed by the Chinese imperial families. Historians are interested solely in the role the eunuchs played in the politics of China, the harm they wrought, or the kind of trouble they caused in the fall of any particular state, and they record these facts. However, we who are concerned with cultural history or with anthropology find it of great interest to know in

publication of scholarly works. The series referred to is Dai kōkai jidai sōsho [Collected records of the age of the great navigators].

what way the institution of the eunuchs was distributed on the Eurasian continent, and why it did not cross the Tsushima Straits and enter Japan. Anthropologists have written about this in relation to other questions, as in Alfred Kroeber's monograph on ancient *oikumenē*.[15] I myself think that the Asian nomads included among their pastoral skills knowledge of how to castrate male livestock, and that there may be some connection between this and the Chinese institution of eunuchs. The Greek Herodotus writes of how the Persian royal court, in the pre-Christian, that is, the pre-Islamic, era, employed eunuchs. It is said that Grecian merchants provided the eunuchs. In Egypt and Mesopotamia, parts of the ancient Orient, the royal courts used the institution of eunuchs. In China, there is documentary evidence of eunuchs in each age from the Spring and Autumn to the Warring States, and in the Ch'in and Han Ages. According to scholars, even in the shell-bone inscriptions of the Yin sites there are hieroglyphs that appear to represent the existence of eunuchs. It may be difficult to obtain accurate evidence, but I think there is ample proof.

At any rate, the institution of eunuchs seems to have spread in very ancient times in the cultural spheres of the Eurasian continent. Even in the Christian era, in the palaces of the Eastern Roman Empire, or the Byzantine Empire, a great number of eunuchs were employed. Further, when we come to the Islamic period, history tells us how, from the Mogul Empire of India in the east to the Osman Turks of the twentieth century, there were thousands of eunuchs in the palaces of the Islamic countries. Again, in Western Europe, though there was no institution of eunuchs in the royal palaces, there were eunuch-like men in the royal choirs. This continued until the papacy prohibited it in the nineteenth century.

In China there were eunuchs at the court in

15. "The Greeks had a name for the central area of higher civilization: *oikumenē*. Literally, this meant 'the inhabited world' or civilization as a whole. . . . This *oikumenē* of the Greeks, which stretched from Gibraltar to India and dimly known China, was the region in which people lived in cities in organized states, plowed their fields and raised cattle, worked iron and knew letters" (A. L. Kroeber, *Anthropology* [rev. ed.; New York: Harcourt, Brace and Co., 1948], p. 423). See also the monograph on *oikumenē* by Kroeber entitled *The Ancient Oikumenē as an Historic Culture Aggregate* (Huxley Memorial Lecture for 1945; London: Royal Anthropological Institute of Great Britain and Ireland, 1946). In *Anthropology*, Kroeber remarks that, in spite of the great Chinese influence upon Japanese culture, certain Chinese cultural items were never adopted. Among such practices were eunuchism, foot-binding, the wearing of body jewelry other than in the hair, and opium-smoking. Foot-binding and eunuchism may have "clashed with an unconscious Japanese pattern to which anything like mutilation was repugnant" (p. 417).

Peking until the early twentieth century, and in Korea, in the palace of the Yi dynasty, eunuchs were abundantly employed. In fact, one of the last of the eunuchs of the Yi dynasty is still living. It is said that near Seoul there was a special village which provided the palace with eunuchs. Thus the institution of eunuchs, which extended across the Eurasian continent spreading even to Western Europe, existed also in the Korean peninsula but finally did not cross the Tsushima Straits and enter Japan. This also is a very interesting phenomenon in cultural history. Leaving aside any attempt to explain this, we can nonetheless use the line of the Tsushima Straits as a criterion for comparing the culture of the Japanese with those of other peoples.

Is a Division between East and West Possible?

Next, there is the line joining the Bosporus with the Mediterranean, which forms the boundary between East and West in European eyes. In terms of cultural history, this became a major boundary with the beginning of the age in which Islam confronted Christianity. For Europeans living in the age of the Crusades, the Orient was the Islamic world, such as appeared in the Arabian Nights, and India was wrapped in a veil of mystery. With the founding of the Yuan dynasty, the excursions of Marco Polo, and increasing travel between East and West, China and Japan came to be included in the East. But from our point of view as Japanese, we find it impossible to regard Asia as a single entity, "the Orient." On the contrary, compared with the diversity of the civilizations of Asia, the civilization of the West or of Europe seems to be a single entity.

A group of Finno-Ugric languages, which are of different lineage from the Indo-European languages, survive like islands in Finland and Hungary. However, the majority of the European countries constitute a single cultural sphere conquered by people speaking Indo-European languages, who divided into many subgroups in the not too distant past. The history of the conquest of the areas extending from Iran to India in the east and from the Mediterranean to Europe in the west is not so old. The European nations share cultural elements inherited from these early people speaking Indo-European languages. Christianity entered as a branch of Judaism, the classical civilization of the Greeks was transmitted by the Roman Empire, and the prototype of modern Europe was constructed. Thus, the cultural structure of Europe is far more homogeneous than that of Asia, and there is ample reason for summing it up in the phrase "Western Europe." But it would be impossible to sum up Asia in the same sense with the phrase "the East." A comparison of Japan, China, and India also should make it clear that Asia is a collection of extremely different cultural elements. For one thing, the languages of each of these countries are of completely different lineage. Japanese is thought to be an Altaic language, and Chinese has a linguistic structure entirely different from the Altaic languages. In India, Indo-European languages are predominant, and in the provinces countless old native dialects survive. Religion is not uniform either. The story is often told of a Japanese university professor of natural sciences who attended the oral examination of an Indian student in Japan, and asked him, "Do you often go to a Buddhist temple?" The Indian student could not understand the question and looked mystified. For India is not a Buddhist country, although the Japanese think that because Buddha was born in India the Indians must be Buddhists. The areas in Asia where Buddhists are plentiful are Japan, China, and parts of Southeast Asia. Then, since China is a Buddhist country, it might be thought that China has the same kind of culture as Japan, but in fact its culture is very different. If we compare the Buddhism of China with that of Japan, we discover that there were great differences between the original character of the religion and its character after its transmission to Japan and its permeation among the people. The spiritual life of the Chinese farmer, in contrast to that of the Japanese, is dominated by the fundamental elements of religion such as those represented by Taoism, or those from which Taoism itself emerged. Furthermore, if we compare the formation of the peoples of the three countries, we find that the historical conditions also differ. There is no doubt that the civilizations of China and India were transmitted to Korea and Japan, but one cannot say that Asia is one simply because of this. To think of Asia as a single cultural sphere is meaningless.

The concept of the West can be justified, but the concept of the East as the area beyond the line drawn from the Mediterranean to the Bosporus, and thus dividing the Eurasian continent geographically in this way, has little practical significance from an academic standpoint. Then, if we approach the West from Japan, approximately where do we become conscious of "the West"? When I left Japan, I found that in Southeast Asia I could sense something akin to Japan in ways of life based upon wet rice culture and in the racial predominance of Mongoloid characteristics. But once in India and Pakistan, beyond the national boundary of Burma, there was an alien quality which made me feel that I had entered a foreign country. Chie Nakane,[16] like myself an anthropologist, has reported similar observations in the *Japan Quarterly*. Also, Mme Alva Myrdal, a sociologist and the present Swedish Ambassador to India, after traveling from India through Burma and Thailand to Japan, described her experience of feeling "the East" as soon as she

16. 1926—. Cultural anthropologist; the first woman to become a full professor at the University of Tokyo. Her writings include studies of India, where Miss Nakane conducted field research, and studies of Japanese social structure. See Bibliography.

had crossed the boundary from India into Burma. These experiences could be supported by evidence drawn from the various cultural elements and the cultural lineage theories we have discussed, but in any case this feeling common to people from both East and West is proof of the problem posed by this boundary line.

The Comparative Culture Studies Approach

In our country there have been many studies of Japanese culture and its distinctive qualities. In particular, writers for intellectual magazines have held lively discussions on Japanese culture. In contrast, discussions of this kind among Europeans— such as the English becoming conscious of English culture and discussing it, or the French debating the elements of French culture—seem to be far fewer. In Japan, however, since the Meiji era, Japanese culture has been earnestly debated, perhaps because of the special circumstances in which Japan found herself. For example, if we look at the table of contents of the book entitled *Kokumin-sei jukkō* [Ten lectures on the national character], written by Yaichi Haga[17] in 1907, we find the following items:

1. Loyalty to superiors and patriotism
2. Reverence for ancestors and respect for the family name
3. Realistic and this-worldly sentiment
4. Love for trees and flowers, and delight in nature
5. A happy and humorous temperament
6. Simplicity and neatness
7. A delicate elegance and ingenuity
8. Love of cleanliness and purity
9. Attachment to ceremony and etiquette
10. Kindliness and magnanimity[18]

17. 1867–1927. A scholar of Japanese literature whose works include reference books on Japanese classical literature and reforms in textbooks of Japanese literature.

18. Translation taken from the introduction to A. L. Sadler's *A Short History of Japan* (London: Angus and Robertson, 1963).

This is a list full of virtues, which means, I suppose, that the Japanese are a truly fine people. Haga discusses each of these traits, giving a great many examples. Now, while I do not deny that these may be justifiable, to catalogue the distinctive traits of the Japanese or of Japanese culture as has been done in many books is not a satisfactory approach.

Instead, I would like to consider Japanese culture with the following questions in mind. When the opposition between the Eastern and Western civilizations becomes more intense in the future international environment, in what ways will the so-called Japanese traits or Japanese national character change, and should such change be welcomed or resisted? Writing in the Meiji era, Haga raised the following questions. With the influx of Western civilization into Japan, the civilizations of East and West have influenced each other and are beginning to harmonize. It is in our country that this blending of the two has most clearly taken place. In these circumstances how long can our national character be preserved? He gives the following examples. Some Japanese now do not pay respect to the gods; children bring lawsuits over property against their parents; some homes have no Shinto altar for offerings; and some husbands use the polite suffix "-san" when speaking to their wives. And he laments, "In this age of transition, what will appear next, a Buddha or a demon?" The times make one think of a magician's box, he continued. The virtues of an individual are also his shortcomings. Inevitably the defects of our people lie latent in their virtues. Since we have entered the international arena, we must be prepared for this. What has to be changed must be changed. What should be preserved must be preserved.

This kind of consciousness of cultural issues pervades the whole of this work. Haga had a thorough knowledge of Europe and was a fine

scholar well versed in world trends. I too share
the consciousness of Haga's *Kokumin-sei jukkō*.
However, I approach the problem from the standpoint of the study of comparative culture. I am
trying to make an academic analysis of the relation
among the formation of the Japanese people, the
origins of Japanese culture, and the cultural distinctiveness of the present-day Japanese. I also hope
to raise questions on the future of Japanese culture.
However, I lack the knowledge and information
on Japanese folklore necessary to support my thesis.
There would, I think, be great value in the research
of scholars of folklore who were aware of these
problems, and who could analyze the nature of
our culture as expressed in the traditions of the
common people of Japan and in the "personality"
of the farmer. My approach raises many issues,
each of which might well be taken up as an object
of study by folklore scholars.

Now I would like to consider what milieu has
contributed to the origins and history of the distinctive traits of Japanese culture which I have felt
and which many scholars have pointed out. I would
like to discover whether there is some kind of basic
structural relationship among the distinctive character traits that appear to be discrete factors. For
instance, research in folklore could cover a single
village or town, or the whole of Japan, and certain
traditional factors could be noted and recorded.
Consequently, one fruitful path would be to carry
out an analysis in the field of Japanese folklore from
the standpoint of tracing the structural correlation
among various cultural elements such as the family
institution, the concept of the gods, beliefs, legends,
and folklore. As I mentioned before, this is what
I would like to see done in the field of Japanese
folklore studies. Now, since I am thinking of two
categories of clues, one from cultural history and
the other from the structure of culture, related to

the distinctiveness of Japanese culture and its comparison with Western civilization, I would like to discuss these next.

The Distinctive Traits of a Rice-Growing Cultural Sphere

As I have mentioned several times, one clue to the distinctiveness of Japanese culture is that it belongs to the rice-growing cultural sphere characterized by irrigated rice cultivation. I think this is a basic factor from beginning to end. In general, the area in which irrigated rice cultivation is conducted, though it has now extended nearly to New Guinea, covers Indonesia, mainland Southeast Asia, India, southern China, Okinawa, Japan, and southern Korea. Historically, southern China is the center. There is historical evidence for the fact that rice growing spread widely in these areas centering around the specific region known as the monsoon belt, where extremely warm and humid air brings seasonal rain. Of course, branching out from this monsoon belt, a few areas of rice production have recently developed in northern China and in Manchuria. Technological progress has been able to conquer climatic and soil conditions to this extent. Even in cold Hokkaidō, irrigated rice production is practiced, but the original irrigated rice-producing areas of Japan fell mainly within the monsoon belt. It is inconceivable that this fact could be irrelevant to the nature of Japanese culture.

The inhabitants of the monsoon belt share a set of skills in daily life based on rice-cultivation techniques, with the accompanying agricultural rites concerning rice, or animistic concepts that embody consciousness of universal phenomena as expressions of life. Again it is clear that the inhabitants of the monsoon belt are highly responsive to the humidity of the environment,[19] as was long ago pointed out

19. "The distinctive character of human nature in the monsoon zone can be understood as submissive and resignatory. It is the humidity that reveals this character" (Tetsuro Watsuji, *Climate and Culture*, trans. Geoffrey Bownas [Tokyo: Hokuseido Press, 1970], p. 20). The Japanese title, *Fūdo*, translated as "a climate," indicates a milieu and signifies cultural values. The wet climate of the monsoon zone was suitable for rice cultivation, which needs many hands, and this led to the development of the family system and closely knit communities. Wheat culture is associated with a pastoral economy.

in Tetsuro Watsuji's *Climate and Culture*. Needless to say, these factors are deeply connected with Japanese culture.

I often use the phrases "agrarian culture" and "nomadic culture." Agrarian culture is widespread, found throughout the world. If we take the vast area of the African and Eurasian continents, the wheat- and oat-cultivating sphere covers almost the whole of Europe to the west and extends into China, Korea, and Manchuria in the east. In contrast to the size of this wheat-growing sphere, the areas of irrigated rice production are limited to the monsoon belt. Therefore it may be possible to divide the agrarian cultural sphere roughly into a wheat culture zone and a rice culture zone.

At the same time, within the same monsoon cultural zone where the basis of life is irrigated rice cultivation, the question of the line of the Tsushima Straits arises, as discussed above. What connection does this have with the influx of a higher civilization from China, India, or Korea? We have considered how archaeologically southern Korea and western Japan in the Yayoi and Tomb Ages, although on opposite sides of the Tsushima Straits, for a long time shared the characteristics of what could be classified as almost a single cultural sphere. It seems likely that the traditions of the historic age just mentioned and of the prehistoric age—the traditions of the Jōmon culture people—have been strongly influential in drawing a definite line in later history between the people of Korea and the people of Japan at the Tsushima Straits. This is obvious from the point of view of language but it can also be seen in the life of the people.

Consequently, Japanese culture belongs to a very large agrarian cultural sphere, or to the set of agrarian culture zones that developed along the southern borders of the Eurasian continent. Further, Japanese culture belongs to the cultures of a set of areas practicing irrigated rice production in the monsoon

belt of this agrarian culture sphere. The question
now arises of the line between India and Burma.
Even though irrigated rice production may have
entered India in the fairly distant past, we may
nonetheless draw this line separating areas of rice
production from other areas around here. The third
point is that what can be defined as the distinctively
Japanese culture is the culture of the area inhabited
by the Japanese, separated from the rest of Asia by
the line of the Tsushima Straits. Thus, in view of all
these aspects, the first clue would be to consider the
relationship between Japanese agriculture, the basis
of living, together with the life style of the farmers,
and the distinctiveness of Japanese culture today.

The "Secluded Stability" of Japanese Culture

The second clue is, as mentioned before, the fact
that, even before the establishment of the Yamato
court, the superior culture of the continent, together
with the people bearing that culture, had several
times entered the Japanese islands from western
Japan. We can hypothesize that the rice-growing
culture of the Yayoi Age or the culture of the northern equestrian people in the middle Tomb Age
entered Japan on the wave of some kind of population movement. To what extent this outside contact
was a large-scale movement of conquest as maintained in the equestrian people theory is not yet
known, but movements of alien peoples or conquests certainly fall within the range of possibilities.
However, since at least the Nara period, for a
period of a thousand and several hundred years, the
Japanese people have developed an increasingly
homogeneous culture without experiencing any
large-scale movement of peoples from outside or
invasion and subsequent conquest by an enemy.
This is an indisputable fact of Japanese history.

After World War II, we experienced for the first time an occupation by a foreign army, but previously, since at least the time of the formation of the Japanese state, we had never once had such an experience. This reflects Japan's special geographic features; military power often infiltrated Korea but always stopped short of the line of the Tsushima Straits. History records some slight infiltration along the Japan Sea, but there was no occupation such as the holding of some corner of Japan by a foreign power, nor were there any military activities. The Mongolian invasion of Kublai Khan[20] consisted merely of the landing of forces in Kyūshū, and the invaders, overwhelmed by the so-called *kamikaze*,[21] withdrew without occupying Japan. This kind of history has given Japanese culture a character which Takeo Kuwahara[22] refers to as "secluded stability." For more than a thousand years, in spite of regional diversity, the Japanese people conducted relations solely among themselves within a single national unit and experienced no contact with foreign countries. In a recent issue of the periodical *Nihon* [Japan], Yoshio Masuda[23] published an essay entitled "Nihon bunka no junsui-sei" [The purity of Japanese culture], in which he defined Japanese culture using the word "purity." The critics often use such phrases as "a mixed culture," and other anthropologists as well as myself hold the view that the composition of Japanese culture is complex and diverse, assimilating with ease European civilization or whatever else, so that Japanese culture is composed of various alien elements. There are ample grounds for such a view, but, on the other hand, compared to Europeans the Japanese provide a rare case, not to be found elsewhere, of a people maintaining an astonishing homogeneity from ancient times, even while assimilating such alien elements, and remaining quite complacent in the process.

When we turn to Europe, we see that it has often experienced large-scale invasions from Asia. Fur-

20. 1215?–94. Mongol emperor, founder of the Yüan dynasty of China (1260–1368). After conquering China and Korea, Kublai Khan attempted to subdue Japan. In 1274, an invasion was undertaken by about 30,000 Mongols and Koreans, but they were driven back when a storm arose. In 1281, a second attack, made by a force of an estimated 140,000 men, ended after two months of fighting with another storm and the break-up of the vast enemy expedition.

21. The term *kamikaze* (divine wind), used in reference to the timely intervention of the storms, was also used in World War II to describe the Japanese suicide corps of air pilots. The temples and shrines which had played their role in sutra readings and incantations to ward off the Mongolian invasions claimed that the Japanese gods (*kami*) had protected the nation. The Mongolians had crossed over from Korea to Kyūshū in the typhoon season, but their defeat was attributed to divine intervention, and *kamikaze* became a synonym for certain victory.

22. 1904—. A scholar of Western cultural history whose writings include studies of French literature and works of literary criticism.

23. 1928—. Cultural anthropologist whose writings include works on Latin American ethnology and ethnohistory.

thermore, among the Europeans themselves, first the Roman Empire consolidated the entire realm, then the northern Celts and the German peoples appeared, frequently advancing on Rome, and the Indo-European peoples who entered Europe built states here and there. Also, more than a thousand years, close to two thousand years, of internecine struggles have taken place among European nations and peoples. Conquest and occupation were matters of daily occurrence, and the peoples of Europe have repeatedly had cultures forced upon them from outside and have reacted just as often against this. In contrast to this pattern of Western civilization, Japanese culture has not met the hardships of invasion and conquest but has developed in sheltered security. That is why in the period of the Warring States, when there was slight contact with Western civilization, the Japanese enthusiastically adopted anything that was unusual or that might be of advantage, assuming that since they had money they should purchase it, and that they would someday find it of use. According to the records of the Spanish missionaries which I mentioned before, in the age of Hideyoshi[24] even Japanese who were not Christian carried the rosaries used in the Christian services as accessories, or wore velvet Western costumes, or used the crucifix as a decoration. In fact, they accepted these as the contemporary fashion, and this kind of phenomenon can be seen from the sixteenth century onward. So eclectic were they that the story is told of a present-day Japanese going to Europe and saying with admiration, "Why even in the West they decorate Christmas trees!" This characteristic of the Japanese appeared clearly during the period of the Warring States. Since long ago the Japanese have been sensitive to alien cultures and have immediately assimilated them. As to where this energy of the Japanese comes from, I am not yet prepared to answer.

24. 1536–98. Hideyoshi completed the unification of Japan, a task begun by Nobunaga, his lord (daimyō). He made himself the ruler of Japan, assuming the title of imperial regent, and conducted domestic reforms which laid the foundations for the society over which the Tokugawa ruled. His interest in foreign trade and attempted conquest of Korea are characteristic of the energy of the sixteenth-century Japanese, who resembled their English counterparts of Elizabethan times in their overseas activities.

The period of the Warring States (Sengoku) extended from the beginning of the Ōnin War in 1467 to the entrance of Nobunaga into Kyoto in 1568, which marks the beginning of the unification of Japan after constant warfare between rival daimyō.

The Endogamous Tradition and
the Vitality of the Japanese

The problem of "secluded stability" or "purity" is one we should regard as a distinctive characteristic of Japanese culture, in spite of the rapid assimilation of foreign cultures. In fact, it may be because of this seclusion and purity that it was possible for the Japanese to continue to assimilate foreign cultures so rapidly without anxiety.

We often use the word "endogamy" in anthropology. In Japan, the institution of selecting a mate from within a certain group such as a community, village, or kinship group is called *zokunai-kon* or *naikon-sei*. If we apply this concept to Japan, we find that Japan as a nation or the Japanese as a whole are an extremely "endogamous" people. There is a general trend for peoples who practice exclusively kinship marriage or endogamy gradually to lose their racial vitality and vigor, but this is not the case with the Japanese. They have what appear to be the strangely inconsistent characteristics of being endogamous as a people, yet being able to assimilate rapidly new cultural elements from outside. Perhaps this is what has maintained the people's youthful vitality.

There is a form of questionnaire called the "social distance scale," devised by an American sociologist, Emory Stephen Bogardus, as a method of calculating statistically the psychological distance among different races or different peoples by posing eleven questions. Among these questions are the following: members of which nationality or race would you invite to your home, or associate with as friends, or not mind sharing a room with? The final question is, "If your sister chose to marry a member of a certain nationality or certain race, would you oppose this, or not?" A graduate student in cultural anthropology at the University of Tokyo did a study on present-day Japanese college students for his master's thesis, adopting this method of research to find out what the Japanese thought of the different peoples of the world. Through this study, he discovered that students today do not mind eating with or associating with people of other nationalities, but when it comes to the question of marriage, the overwhelming majority answer no. The figures for negative responses from Japanese students with regard to marriages with members of other nationalities and other races were surpassed only by the frequency of negative answers of American whites with respect to marriage with Negroes. Thus, even the Japanese of the younger generation today, who have more opportunity to meet foreigners and who have developed, it is said, an international outlook, are still extremely negative with regard to the question of participating in international marriages. This phenomenon is convincing evidence of how the entire Japanese people share a tradition of endogamy. Many reasons can be given for this, the first of which is that Japan is an island country somewhat distant from the nearest continent. The royal families and dynasties of different European nations which have contiguous territories on the continent were all interrelated. When we compare the statistics of such countries with the data on Japan (research data on other Asian nations are not available, so this unfortunately becomes a comparison with only the nations of Western civilization), we find that the Japanese are extremely negative with regard to international marriages with other peoples. This comes out very clearly in the above study of the younger generation, and it is a characteristic that contrasts sharply with the European cultural sphere.

European Logic and the Basis of Japanese Culture

It can perhaps be seen from the above that one characteristic of the Japanese people is that they do not pursue any issue to its logical conclusion, or make exhaustive inquiries into any problem; in fact there is even a tendency to undervalue such approaches. The Japanese are often said to be illogical, but according to the traditional Japanese consciousness, logic is not necessarily highly valued. Respect for logic is an attitude that entered Japan only after the Meiji Restoration, along with standards of Western civilization. The natural sensibility of the Japanese placed value not on logicality but on illogicality or suprarationality. Also, the Japanese do not emphasize the European logical premises which claim to classify and categorize objects. The Japanese mode of thought does not set up classifications and categories such as good and evil, self and other, subject and object, man and nature, or life and death with which to structure concepts.

Consequently, as Takeo Kuwahara has said, logic and rhetoric did not develop in Japan. The Japanese were not faced with the necessity of developing a Western type of logic or rhetoric. In an extremely endogamous society, understanding did not depend on talking; instead, communication was possible through the shared Japanese understanding, without words. Japanese politicians even today approve of communicating by methods such as hara-gei[25] and ishin-denshin.[26] In effect, the Japanese do not value rhetoric, or oratory that appeals to people by persuasion based on logical argument, or moving one's opponent with a show of eloquence. On the contrary, an orator is felt to be shallow and contemptible.

The universities still have debating societies, and debating forums are held. But whether because the oratory of politicians is not much esteemed, or for

25. The concept of hara-gei (hara means literally stomach or belly but in this case mind, intention, spirit; gei means art, accomplishments) is defined by Robert J. C. Butow as follows: "A man who uses hara-gei is a man who says one thing but means another" (Robert J. C. Butow, Japan's Decision to Surrender [Stanford: Stanford University Press, 1954], p. 70, n. 48). Butow analyzes this "art of bluffing" and gives examples of hara-gei. George Akita also examines this concept in his Foundations of Constitutional Government in Modern Japan, 1868–1900 (Cambridge: Harvard University Press, 1967), pp. 139–40. For the significance of the concept of hara to the Japanese, see Karlfried Graf von Dürckheim, The Japanese Cult of Tranquillity, trans. Eda O'Shiel (London: Rider and Co., 1960), pp. 39–40. Dürckheim writes: "The Japanese has a special word for the centre of body and soul: Hara. The number of expressions in which it is found indicates its importance for him. There are master schools that make hara the sole object of their exercise, while every master art in Japan considers it is necessary to possess it in order to achieve 'success' in whatever one is doing. To the Japanese, what a man experiences in the 'centre of being' is none other than the unity of life. . . ." Dürckheim has also written a monograph on hara, entitled Hara: The Vital Center of Man, translated by Sylvia-Monica von Kospoth, in collaboration with Estelle R. Healey (London: Allen and Unwin, 1962).

Political parties in Japan are, in effect, families, which explains the attitude of politicians who use hara-gei tactics.

26. Tacit or intuitive understanding; communication between mind and mind. This can be compared to the explicit modes of

some other reason, we do not find their speeches attractive. However, in Europe, since the Greek and Roman ages, oratory has been regarded as an indispensable qualification for an intellectual, especially for a statesman. It was a premise of democracy that statesmen present their principles in the forum before the assembled citizens and thus endeavor to persuade them.

To some extent, this European tradition opens up opportunities for the emergence of demagogues. Hitler, in order to appeal to the masses, took instruction from the leading German stage actors, and practiced everything from diction upward. It is said that he polished every speech to the utmost, from phrasing to intonation. In comparison to this, in Japan, though it is said that parliamentary government has developed and that an age of democracy has arrived, oratory is far inferior to that of Europe. In the period of the "movement for democratic rights"[27] or the period of Taishō democracy,[28] there appeared politicians in the European sense of the word, like Yukio Ozaki,[29] but this kind of tradition has almost wholly disappeared by now. I have not heard any attractive speeches made by present-day politicians, and this too, I think, is related to the bases of Japanese culture.

Now, at this point, I think it may be possible to make a scholarly ethno-linguistic analysis of the question of the Japanese language, mentioned before, which is closely connected with the question of Japanese culture. For instance, I often say, "Naninani nano da ga" ["It is such-and-such, but . . ."]. This conjunction "ga" which we Japanese use a great deal raises a question. In Japanese, sentences, phrases, and clauses are linked together with "ga." When translating this "ga" into English, "but" sounds strange, yet "and" does not convey the proper meaning. No matter which European language we select, it is almost impossible to convey the meaning of the conjunction "ga" in its real sense.

communication necessary in a heterogeneous society such as that of America.

27. A movement demanding democratic rights from the oligarchic government in the early Meiji years. In 1880 the leaders formed organizations, and later political parties, calling for a parliamentary system. Under pressure, the government arranged for the establishment of constitutional government by gradual stages. The Meiji Constitution was promulgated in 1889.

28. During the Taishō period (1912–26), Japan's increasingly urban and industrialized society made new demands upon politics. Expansion of suffrage and welfare legislation were sought by socialist political movements. The early 1920s have been regarded as a time of growing democracy and party government.

29. 1859–1954. An outstanding liberal politician and political critic who helped in the formation of the Kaishintō (Progressive Party) in 1882, and criticized the oligarchs' government. He was elected to every diet from 1890 to 1952 and served as minister of justice in the Okuma cabinet and as mayor of Tokyo. He fought for universal manhood suffrage and took an antimilitarist stand during the 1930s and World War II. His gift of cherry trees to Washington, D.C., is well known.

In Japan there is a distinctive and vague use of words in daily life which does not obey the rules of logic. Indeed one may say that this use maintains Japanese personal relations. For example, should a Japanese husband say to his wife, "Shall we go to see a movie today or a play?" a Japanese woman, even if she wanted to see a movie, might say, "Well, I would like to see a movie, but . . ." ending with an uncertain note as if to yield the decision to her husband. If she were a Westerner, she would probably say clearly, "I want to go to a movie," or "I don't want to go," and give a definite yes or no. From the Westerner's point of view, the Japanese are inscrutable because they do not say yes or no clearly. The Westerner declares that he cannot understand what the Japanese is really thinking. Also the so-called Japanese smile, that is, the Japanese custom of smiling when a situation is not funny, is incomprehensible to the Westerner. Some Westerners, looking puzzled, even ask why the Japanese think the situation is funny. This kind of gap in understanding between the Japanese and the Westerner is closely connected to the question of the structure of the culture. These are all questions that can become the object of scholarly analysis. In particular, those who pursue the study of Japanese folklore should not be satisfied with merely investigating the rituals of a village, or the relation between the god of the mountain and the god of the paddy fields. With this kind of knowledge as a basis, the problems I have mentioned—discovering what underlies a people's culture, and how to grasp this in a scholarly way and analyze it structurally—should become the objects of study in the future.

In the next chapter, I want to develop these topics a little further by focusing on a comparison of East and West, limiting the East to Japan, and comparing Japan with Europe or the European cultural sphere.

6. Japan and the West

Changes in Views of the West: The Meiji Restoration and the Recent Defeat

It goes without saying that, in the period of modernization that followed the Meiji Restoration of 1868, Europe or Europe and America, namely, the West, became of great concern to the generation of our immediate ancestors. At that time, it was a matter of vital importance for the Japanese to catch up with the civilization of the Western powers. From the standpoint of Japan, the West was in every respect advanced and civilized, and Japan in comparison was an extremely backward Asian nation. It is also obvious that our ancestors, spurred by their consciousness of their country's backwardness, absorbed Western civilization with great rapidity. Especially in technological fields, the fact that within one century Japan caught up with the revolution which had taken Western Europe over five centuries to achieve is an indication that for the Japanese people there was no other course of action. In the early years of the Meiji era, it was an accepted fact for the Japanese that European civilization had to be their model. This tradition of following the West persisted into the subsequent Taishō and Shōwa eras and continues even today.

For example, Erwin Baelz[1] wrote in a letter dated the ninth year of Meiji [1876], "(. . . here I come to the strangest feature of the situation) the Japanese . . . are impatient when a word is said of their past. The

1. 1849–1913. A German scholar of internal medicine who, in 1876, was appointed instructor in physiology at the Tokyo Medical School. He lectured on general pathology, taught until 1902, and contributed to the development of Japanese medical science.

Baelz's journal, quoted in the text, throws light upon conditions in the late nineteenth century in Japan; see *Awakening Japan: The Diary of a German Doctor*, ed. Toku Baelz, trans. Eden and Cedar Paul (New York: Viking, 1932).

cultured among them are actually ashamed of it."
He went on as follows, describing a conversation
with some Japanese acquaintances: " 'That was in
the days of barbarism,' said one of them in my
hearing. Another, when I asked him about Japanese
history, bluntly rejoined: 'We have no history. Our
history begins today.' " It was this kind of consciousness that made possible the rapid modernization of the Meiji era and produced a cultural revolution in ways of living in Japan.

However, recently in Japan, since the experience
of World War II, as contacts with Western civilization have become closer, there has appeared a series
of critiques of Western civilization which form a
contrast to the views of the West held since the
Meiji era. One representative example is the critique
of Western civilization made by Yūji Aida, professor of Western history at Kyoto University, who
spent two years as a prisoner of the English on the
Burmese front. Aida has published a series of papers
beginning with *Ahlone shūyōjo* [The Ahlone camp],
in which, from the standpoint of a historian of the
West, he examines the limitations of Western
humanism, ways of life, and survival and analyzes
the historical bases of European culture and Japanese
culture. His views deserve consideration. Readers of
Ahlone shūyōjo will recall that Aida has made penetrating observations on both the virtues and shortcomings of the English with whom he was in close
contact, and of Western civilization as seen through
the medium of England, based upon his own experiences as a prisoner of the English. His views
form a marked contrast to the traditional European-
centered outlook of the Japanese. Aida personally
had an extremely strong hatred of the English. He
even wrote that while he was a prisoner he felt that
the world would be a better place to live in if the
English vanished from the face of the earth.

Thus, some Japanese have expressed feelings about
Western civilization totally different from those of

the Japanese who talked to Baelz. The critic Michio
Takeyama, a scholar of German literature, has made
a shrewd analysis of Christianity itself, a constituent
element of Western civilization. Starting with the
question whether European nations can be called
Christian nations, he argues that a tragedy such as
that symbolized by the gas chambers of the Nazis
has a deep relationship with Christianity. Furthermore, basing his conclusions on a detailed analysis
of the Bible and other works, he has pointed out the
traditional anti-Semitism of Western civilization
springing from the concept of "punishment for the
Jews."

"In Germany There Was No Midwar Generation"

Recently, the critic Hyōye Murakami has written
an analysis of Western civilization, especially of
Germany, drawing on impressions formed during
his European travels. It expresses frankly how Japanese sensibility reacts against Western civilization.

There is no space to introduce all the details here,
but I would like to point out where his line of
reasoning agrees with mine. Murakami's article is
entitled "In Germany There Was No Midwar
Generation" (Chūō kōron, December 1965). He also
appended the subtitle "Is the Concept of the Midwar
Generation a Sentimentalism Peculiar to the Japanese? A Consideration of the Sources and Differences of the Civilizations of the East and the West."
The article begins with the subheading "The Gap
One Feels between Eastern and Western Culture."
Murakami's main desire in Europe was to find out
whether among the German intellectuals there was
anything that corresponded to the so-called midwar
generation and its characteristic sensibilities in Japan.
Although he went with the latent hope of confirm-
ing the existence of this pattern in Germany, he

slowly became aware of the differences between Eastern and Western cultures and the chasm that separates them.

In Japan, the phrase "midwar generation" appeared in response to the moral question of war guilt. Regardless of whether one had cooperated with or resisted the war effort, the extreme experiences of wartime all seemed to have been in vain after the war. The slogan "American and English devils" was replaced by the saying "The repentance of a hundred million," and the inscription on the Hiroshima Peace Memorial, "We shall not repeat this mistake." The generation that had keenly felt this swift change in the Japanese mentality and the emptiness which came from regarding the war and cooperation in the war effort as mistakes had found their doubts aroused when they were blamed, and their doubts were quickly followed by feelings of indignation and by soul-searching. All these intermingled in their daily consciousness and became cause for introspection. These people, now between the ages of forty and fifty, are called the midwar generation in Japan.

In contrast to Japan, Germany not only suffered defeat but also bore the revelation of the shocking facts of the massacre of six million Jews by the Nazis. Nonetheless, Murakami describes how the Japanese intellectual, in going to Germany expecting to find that the unbearable emotions of the intellectuals who witnessed this tragedy have created a midwar generation with an even greater intensity of feeling than their counterparts in Japan, comes up against the reality that this kind of midwar consciousness hardly exists among the Germans. For thousands of years, upon European soil, nations and peoples have repeatedly shed their blood and others' in asserting their right to survive. Europeans with this kind of historical background assume that it is the people's duty to bear arms in defense of their country. Any questioning of the responsibility of cooperation in a war would immediately be met with counterarguments. Naturally the Japanese find it strange to see how the Germans have held to one consistent attitude with regard to war.

This mode of thought is not peculiar to the Germans but is dominant throughout Europe. Murakami claims that this is because European civilization is the expression of a virile instinct to defend one's own position, claims, and rights, in other words, the bases of one's own survival, and this is what sustains nationalism in Europe. Therefore, he feels that in Japan there is a distinct qualitative difference in the use of this same word "nationalism."

The European Sense of Responsibility

Murakami gives various examples of this. For instance, there is a memorial stone standing at the tip of Cape Soya in Hokkaidō, with an inscription to the effect that this is the northernmost point in Japan, but Japan has not yet abandoned Sakhalin in any official treaty. Thus, even before any treaty has confirmed the fact, the Japanese have marked this place as the actual northernmost limit of their land, making an inscription on a stone monument. In Hiroshima, the inscription reads, "We shall not repeat this mistake," and at the northern tip of Hokkaidō, "The northernmost point in Japan."

However, if we go to Germany, says Murakami, we find that in West Germany the term East Germany is not used, at least in the way we use it. In West Germany, the term East Germany means the Polish territory, including East Prussia, east of the present East Germany which long ago ceased to be German territory. Even in the television weather forecasts, the old boundaries of Germany appear on the screen, and weather is forecast for the whole of

Germany. Further, I have noticed myself that the new names given to territories since World War I never appear in new books. The old names as they were when Germany occupied these territories are used. Even the names of places in Africa and the Pacific that were German colonies are still in use. This is in great contrast to the "good-natured" ways of the Japanese, comments Murakami.

Again, in Germany, after the war there should have been, as a matter of course, a change in the values held by intellectuals. Accordingly, he expected to find among European intellectuals, particularly the Germans, a sense of the gap between the prewar and postwar periods, or frustration such as we Japanese, especially the intellectuals, had experienced, but he was unable to discover such frustration, for this feeling seems to have arisen from Japanese sensibilities. In European culture, there does not exist a sense of responsibility with this connotation. With these reflections, Murakami returned to Japan.

A modern ethic of responsibility based on the individual conscience developed in the West in modern times. We have been accustomed to thinking that in Japan the awakening of individualism has been delayed, and that, accordingly, an ethic of responsibility has not been established, but Murakami began to wonder if the reverse might not be true. For instance, in Europe, even if an accident occurs through a man's own carelessness, he will never acknowledge it. He will argue any other cause but his own carelessness, putting forward even the most preposterous reasons. Japanese trading companies in Germany employing many Germans unanimously hold that this is their most unpleasant trait. However, as Murakami points out, the Germans are merely following their own traditional code of ethics, which says that offenses have to be proved, and proof requires logical argument.

Furthermore, references are often made to Ruth

Benedict's *The Chrysanthemum and the Sword*, in which the author used the phrase "shame culture" to describe the Japanese trait of making other people's opinions the criterion of action. In comparison, she calls the Christian culture of Western civilization, in which the criterion of action lies in an ethic based on a sense of sin vis-à-vis the absolute God, a "guilt culture." But according to Murakami, as for the relation between the actions of Europeans and their code of ethics or sense of sin, it is very doubtful whether they feel any guilt after committing an offense. Immediately, like a reflex action, an inner voice urges them to defend themselves. Self-defense and personal survival are the primary issues. In the case of the Japanese, however, loyalty to the group to which they belong calls forth a deep consciousness of sin. Also among the Japanese, the maintenance of a psychological balance between two factors, namely, that the other party was at fault but that one's own carelessness should also be considered, provides an important method of resolving disputes. However, Europeans carry out matters in an "all or nothing" fashion. Murakami explains that there is a great difference in the way of thinking and feeling about the essense of responsibility.

He then continues, giving examples from literary works. For instance, the Japanese values the words "I am sorry," which express a sense of responsibility, and the emotions that prompt these words, even before he knows how the other party will show his sense of responsibility in deeds. In contrast to this, Europeans are quite indifferent to the existence of any responsibility unaccompanied by appropriate action.

The European Belief in Power

Murakami pursues his line of reasoning further, turning to another aspect of the problem. Europeans have a deeply instinctive belief in and awe of power. Their technique of disciplining children is a good example of this. People say that Japanese children are undisciplined, behaving in an unruly and willful manner because their parents spoil them. Surely there is no other country in the world like this. In Europe and in America, children are strictly disciplined and Japan should learn from this. Of course, to a certain extent, Murakami agrees and he does not think that the present system of child rearing in Japan should be left as it is. He goes on, however, to observe that, although children in the West are so well-mannered that they are really like little gentlemen, quiet like grown-ups, this is true only when grown-ups are watching them. When they come to play in a Japanese home, since the Japanese "spoil" children, European children instantly take advantage and become as unruly as if their character had completely changed. The Japanese housewives in Germany all spoke of how they resented the sham good manners of the German children, who pulled out toys one by one, became absorbed in their play, and would not listen when the Japanese parents asked them to put the toys away. When they were given tasty cakes, they clamored for more and even went and opened the kitchen cupboard to get some. Murakami explains that there was a simple reason for this unruly behavior. The children's bottoms had felt the pain inflicted by their parents', especially their mothers', spankings. In other words, physical discipline was the means of training children in Europe. At street corners, mothers could be seen hauling their crying children about by their ears. This type of physical discipline is very strict in Western societies, and European children are controlled almost entirely by physical pain and fear. Therefore, children become extremely quick to read the moods of grown-ups, and once they see they can take advantage of someone, they become uncontrollable.

Again, since Murakami is a critic, his observations sometimes throw light on interesting things that a scholar might pass by. For instance, he describes how, in the streets of Europe, people—especially women—with dogs are most conspicuous. Sometimes one even sees an old lady walking with a cat on a leash. One cannot help admiring how well trained these pets are. Dogs are seldom seen barking at passersby or at each other, and if they do bark, they quiet down at a sign from their masters. He reflected that this culture in which animal training is so highly developed was an image of the European himself. Training animals requires patience. With the repeated application of physical fear and immediate reward, reflex actions are molded into habits. And this wonderful pattern of animal discipline not only extends to the treatment of children but could also be seen very often in adult society.

He then turns to a comparison of Europe and Japan. The fact that European fruits and vegetables are poor in quality compared with those in Japan reminded him of how the Japanese excel at raising plants. In order to raise plants well, it is necessary to identify with them, to have a feeling of harmony with them. In comparison, when Europeans discipline animals, they force them to obey their will. Perhaps, then, one can say that the distinctive character and the different values of the Japanese and Europeans stem from this. Thus, he came to the conclusion that the European sense of morals is perhaps, in general, different from the Japanese. In Europe, there did not seem to exist any spontaneous sense of morals. A friend who had lived in Europe for three years, recalling Kant's admonition that morality should consist of self-discipline, commented that Kant was probably influenced by the lack of this quality around him. However, in Europe, even though spontaneous morality may be rare, custom is deeply rooted in society, and a custom once established is absolutely followed. For instance, in Europe there are established customs governing table manners and giving one's seat to women in public vehicles, and the maintenance of order in daily life by the observance of these customs is extremely thorough.

German Reflections on the War

Furthermore, Murakami makes the extremely important statement that, even in regard to the cruelties of Nazism exposed after the war, the majority of the Germans may not feel any moral responsibility in the real sense of the word. In this kind of cultural milieu, there does not exist the "humidity" which would nurture either mentally or emotionally the sensibilities of a generation like the Japanese midwar generation.

He explains this as follows. Japan is in the monsoon belt and is a very damp, humid country, but Europe has a dry environment such as Tetsuro Watsuji classified in *Climate and Culture* as a "meadow" environment, and one cannot feel there the humidity that is characteristic of the Japanese and his sensibility. This is why in Europe there is a far higher degree of awe and respect for power and money, taken at their face value, than there is in Japan. This can be seen even in the way people telephone. Let us suppose that the wife of a professor is using the telephone. If the woman were Japanese, she probably would not say, "I am the wife of Professor so-and-so," but a German wife will invariably give all of her husband's titles. If he has the title of doctor, both he and his wife will always use it in letters and on the telephone. This custom seems to have disappeared in England and America, but it is still deeply rooted on the European continent, and it too is quite alien to the Japanese. Although the Japanese are said to be authoritarian in such matters, they consider it a virtue to show restraint and modesty. People would laugh if one said, "This is Commissioner so-and-so's home." Yet not so in Germany. Therefore Murakami writes, "I felt as if the mystery of the social structure that had so readily turned to the massacre of the Jews under Hitler's leadership was slowly being solved for me."

Murakami's article continues. The observation that the Germans seemed to have no compunctions in regard to the war, or even in regard to the Nazis, has been widely made by critics in neighboring countries. This applies to both East and West Germany. I have even heard in West Germany an argument defending Hitler as the first to become aware of the menace of communism, but perhaps this is too extreme to be representative. Nevertheless, one cannot deny that such latent feelings may be unexpectedly widespread. This is related to the traditional German slogan *Deutschland über Alles* ["Germany over all"]. I met a Jewish intellectual in Prague who said laughingly that perhaps even the leaders of East Germany think of Hitler as having been only slightly mistaken. On seeing Germans in the various countries of Eastern Europe walking around with the utmost confidence, one feels inclined to agree with these words. This was something Murakami felt too when he met a close friend who had wholeheartedly supported the Nazis before the war. He sometimes also sensed that friends who were scholars, though they did not openly talk about it, at the bottom of their hearts, far from repenting of the Nazis' actions against the Jews, had the feeling that it would have been just as well if more had been accomplished.

To say this is to invite the rebuttal that such top

German intellectuals as Heinrich Böll and Rolf Hochhuth are pursuing this very question. However, they propose to treat it as one common to all mankind. Certainly this is a theme common to mankind. Nevertheless, before we approach it in this light, we must consider many factors that have sprung specifically from the German national character. At least during this recent trip, Murakami became almost satiated with suggestive whiffs of these elements. He was struck by the rough-and-ready mentality of the Germans who wanted to confront the problem directly from the standpoint of what is common to mankind without examining their own wounds first. This is one conclusion that can be drawn about European civilization as perceived by Japanese sensibilities. Although the case is different, my apprehensions regarding the future of America stem from the knowledge that the Americans too are the heirs to European civilization.

About the time Murakami finished his hundred-day trip, he reread the book *Sekai no seishun* [The youth of the world], which he had carried with him in Germany. In this book of writings left by those who died in World War II, German youths repeatedly describe their despair and discuss the non-existence of God, but he could not find anywhere a single line on the agony of the alienation caused by the gap between themselves and the war aims of their fatherland. The German youth wrote either extraordinarily vivid pieces about the tragedies of the battlefields, or else extremely abstract thoughts about the world in general. Of course, these alone fully expressed the sufferings of youth. However, he could not help recalling the words of Michiko Tanaka,[2] whom he had met in Berlin, to the effect that the Germans had remained unchanged throughout the prewar, midwar, and postwar periods. When he first read *Sekai no seishun* in Japan, his emotions had been particularly stirred by these

2. A Japanese actress who was a longtime resident of Berlin.

writings left by the German war dead. After his trip, however, he was inclined to think that his feelings reflected instead his own "midwar sentiment." Murakami's conclusions are similar to my own line of reasoning, which also agrees with the thinking of Yūji Aida and Michio Takeyama described at the beginning of this chapter.

The Differences between Pastoral Culture and Rice-Based Culture

In the beginning, as a secondary theme, I introduced the experiences of a Japanese reporter who, while living among the Arabian nomadic peoples, discovered how different people could be. I also mentioned his opinion that, if we take Japan and Arabia as the two opposite poles, Europe would be far closer to Arabia. Then, in the paragraphs above, I pointed out Murakami's emphasis on the superiority of Europeans in animal training. In contrast to these Europeans, the Japanese are a people living in a humid climate who cultivate rice with a high level of technical skill and great patience. In effect, the culture of the Japanese people is one of "great humidity and plant-like." Just as it was written in the *Wajin-den* that there were in the land of Wa no domestic animals like cows, horses, or sheep, livestock did not become an established part of life in Japan. Of course, the Japanese may have eaten meat, but livestock became a basis of living and a source of food only after the influence of European civilization began to enter Japan in the Meiji era. In other words, livestock as an element in the traditional life of the Japanese is conspicuously lacking. This is, I think, a definite clue to the understanding of Japanese culture.

By contrast, in Europe, stock breeding has always flourished. Even on the Chinese continent, a far greater amount of stock breeding has been practiced than in Japan. Among the Semitic peoples, the Jews and the Arabs, stock breeding has thrived. The peoples speaking Indo-European languages have also placed far greater emphasis on stock breeding as a basis for livelihood compared to rice-growing peoples. And the nomadic culture of all these peoples has not changed in fundamental character despite the passage of three or four thousand years. Therefore, Western civilization is still strongly pastoral. Naturally agriculture is practiced, but there is a far higher degree of reliance upon stock breeding. For instance, in Homer's *Iliad*, we find in the descriptions of the battles of the Trojan War such metaphors and similes as "black sheep and white sheep mingled together in confusion," or "armies moving like a great flock of sheep." The Japanese war chronicles, however, use imagery based on humidity, such as "like clouds or mists." This is quite natural in a country with a climate as humid as Japan's. Again, when we look up Chinese characters in a work like Tetsuji Morohashi's[3] *The Great Chinese-Japanese Dictionary*, we find that there are a vast number of characters which have as a component part the ideograph for sheep, signifying domestic animals. Even though Chinese civilization belongs to the monsoon zone, it differs greatly from Japan's rice-based culture.

When we analyze Japanese words from this viewpoint, we find that there are very few that have ideographs for animals, particularly domestic animals, as a constituent element. On the other hand, there are many words related to plants. Thus, in my view, the fundamental differences between Western civilization and Japanese culture arise from the differences between pastoral and agricultural, especially rice-based, cultures. Since my opinions on the differences between the two cultures, particularly in their world views, have been published often, I will not refer to them extensively here but will merely point out the main differences.

3. 1883—. A scholar of Confucianism and the Chinese classics who compiled the monumental *Dai-kanwa jiten* [Great Chinese-Japanese Dictionary] in thirteen volumes (1955–60), the culmination of thirty-five years' research.

In considering religion, everyone will recognize the following three religions as monotheistic, namely, Christianity, which spread early in Europe, its matrix, Judaism, and Islam, which was founded somewhat later. These three religions share, in addition to monotheism, a common belief that God exists not within the universe but beyond the universe, as an absolute being. They also share the concept that the universe is the creation of the Absolute, which existed before everything, and the view that everything moves in accordance with the Province of the Absolute. Now, in my opinion, the cultural base for this kind of world view can be found in the sphere of the nomadic peoples extending over the dry plains. With this world view as a foundation, these three world religions developed and, as successors to the tradition of Hebraism, formed one of the important bases for the structure of European civilization.

One other basis of contemporary European civilization is the Greco-Roman tradition. Within Greco-Roman civilization, we find the tradition of the farming cultures of Egypt and of the Aegean civilization, but the peoples who developed and bore this civilization were Aryans. In other words, they were Indo-European peoples. That is why within contemporary European civilization, whose tradition dates back to Greco-Roman times, the common cultural life of the Indo-European peoples persists. In addition, we may recall the warlike German peoples of great vitality who conquered the Roman Empire from the north and are the ancestors of the various peoples now bearing contemporary Western European civilization.

As we look back into world history, we begin to understand the problem of the differences in the historical experiences spanning two or three thousand years, and in the cultures that lie latent in the origins of this history, forming its core. When we try to identify the core of Japanese culture from this viewpoint, we find it finally in the rice-farming pattern of the Yayoi Age, a tradition inherited by the present-day Japanese. Consequently, I have compared the differences between the culture of Europe and of Japan, giving various examples. What I finally wish to emphasize, however, is the difference between the core personalities of the two cultures.

The Idealism of European Civilization

Finally the question left unanswered is whether, after looking at the differences between Western civilization and Japanese culture, we are left with an unbridgeable gap between East and West. Having come as far as this, however, I suspect that we are bound to be skeptical about the existence of this gap. For instance, I do not find any fundamental mistakes in what Murakami described in his article. With the sensibilities of a critic or man of letters, he penetratingly identifies and analyzes an aspect of Western civilization which I myself have also noticed. In particular, I think his point about the Germans is right as far as it goes. However, and this too is based on my own experience, if this gap spoken of by Murakami did exist, it would be impossible to have any profound intercourse with intimate European or American friends, whose cultural background is so different. Although I recognize the existence of this gap, it is contradicted by my experience of such close human relationships.

Furthermore, the same thing can be said of the question of morals and moral character. In regard to the distinction between a shame culture and a guilt culture, or the issue of Christianity, if we confine ourselves to Murakami's views we find that indeed there does not exist in European culture and life the kind of responsibility or virtue that we

Japanese feel. It is certainly true that in European culture human life is sustained by ruthless power, intense self-assertion, and the rigidity of customs which support these.

However, if we pursue the question of whether there exist in Europe moral responsibility and virtue in the sense that we understand them, we cannot deny the profundity of European culture. I should like to discuss this problem at greater length sometime in the future.

Paradoxically, religion and morality seem to emphasize the elements lacking in a culture. In the first chapter, I described several episodes from the series entitled "The Arabian Nomadic Peoples," written by the reporter Honda in the *Asahi*. Here is another illustration from the same series. Honda was talking to a Japanese whose nerves had been worn down by living for several years in Arabia, where the natural environment and people were quite the opposite of what they are in Japan. He said to Honda, "Well, I'd honestly like to see the face of that guy who wrote the song 'The Moonlit Desert.'" So Honda actually went and visited the writer of "The Moonlit Desert," and asked him how he had come to write it. It turned out that this man had never been abroad, let alone to Arabia; he had simply imagined the scene of a prince and princess riding through a moonlit desert on a camel harnessed with gold and silver twine. Then, at the end of this article, Honda describes the following episode, by way of contrast. In a school in Riyadh, many pictures painted by children in the lower grades were hung on the walls. Almost all were paintings of trees with abundant green foliage or of cool water scenery. Of course, in Japan, where water and greenery are plentiful, this would be natural, but just as the scene of a moonlit desert would be unthinkable in Japan, so these scenes are not to be found in Arabia. In the Koran, also, there are descriptions of a paradise where rivers flow copiously. This is the heaven depicted by Mohammed, who was born in the desert town of Mecca. It struck Honda that what the nomadic culture lacked was depicted with passionate desire and idealism.

Again, here is a similar example, though not of nomadic peoples. There is a famous ancient site called Teotihuacán about fifty kilometers northeast of Mexico City, which can be reached by car from the city in less than an hour. Teotihuacán was the site of a very large religious city, and the relics of a strange civilization dating back to around the beginning of the Christian era remain there. In a corner of the ancient city are the vestiges of a sanctuary named Tepantitla, and on the walls of its basement are sacred paintings of the rain deity later known as Tlaloc in the Aztec period, and of the water deity. Also there are paintings in truly beautiful colors of scenes of the paradise imagined by the people of Teotihuacán. The Mexico tableland is a dry region two thousand and several hundred meters above sea level, but the scenes of paradise depicted in the murals are of the tropical scenery east of the Mexican plateau near the Gulf of Mexico. They are scenes of a paradise in which the green foliage of rubber trees flourishes, flowers bloom, birds sing, and waters flow copiously. This too shows us the universal tendency of people to aspire after and idealize far distant things which they themselves lack. The land of Canaan flowing with milk and honey and the paradise depicted in the Koran crossed by abundant rivers are unmistakable proofs of this.

This may seem paradoxical, but perhaps it is because the desert people cannot survive without an aggressive tooth-and-claw self-assertion that a religion of love was born among them. I think we can understand from these examples the inevitability of the emergence among a people whose cultural base is nomadic of an extreme religion of love—with such tenets as "Love your enemies," or "If anyone strikes you on the right cheek, turn to him the other also," or "God is love," absolutely contrary to their own sensibilities in daily living. The European, Indian, and German peoples have almost all been conquered by this religion of the Semites, and today the cultural sphere of Europe and America has become Christian.

When the critic Takeyama, mentioned at the beginning of this chapter, traveled in Europe, he wondered in what sense Europe could be called Christian, or where any vestiges of the Sermon on the Mount could be seen in the Berlin wall dividing East from West or in that barbed-wired city. We may be able to explain this from the standpoint of the idealism within European civilization, which arises from a strong desire to seek that which is lacking. It would surely be a narrow view to pass judgment on European civilization without considering its idealism, basing our opinions instead on only our direct personal experiences.

Spanning East and West

When we Japanese live among Europeans, it is true, as Murakami wrote, that we discover a quality alien to our own sensibilities. On the other hand, the Japanese must be a most mysterious people from the standpoint of the European. A European must feel that they are an unusually alien people. Consequently, if we made a sweeping assertion that European civilization, which developed out of the confluence of various cultural currents, is a world of power confrontations without morality or responsibility, this would violate the standards of academic objectivity.

Perhaps it is difficult for the Japanese to attain a complete understanding of European civilization.

At the same time, we may say that for a European to achieve a real and complete understanding of Japanese culture is also difficult. However, from my own academic standpoint, I think we should study each other's civilizations taking into consideration all the conditions of the data we possess. Then for the first time mutual understanding between East and West would become possible. I think that research on the traditions of intellectual history, such as religion, philosophy, and the arts, and on the elite groups that represent these, along with an investigation of materials drawn from daily life experiences, from politics, from war and military matters, will become increasingly necessary. Furthermore, we should take into consideration the fine virtues and human warmth we feel in our intimate Western friends. One of my European friends who read my essay "A Culture of Love and Hate"[4] commented, "Yes, of course, it is as you say but...," and then added with some embarrassment, "European civilization is not a culture of love and hatred, but a culture that seeks love." According to this friend, European civilization is a culture that ceaselessly pursues the love that is in reality lacking, as I explained previously.

From my own experience in Europe, I think that the line between love and hatred is clearly drawn. In daily life, even scholars are conscious of and quite frankly talk about their enemies or allies. The Japanese, even if they are conscious of this, think it a virtue to smile in front of others and conceal any awareness of opposition. This could not happen in Europe, where favor and disfavor are clearly expressed. Therefore, when we read Western European literature, we feel the passion, vigor, and profundity of the spirit of the European, which plumbs the depth of both hatred and love. This is something we surely must not forget in trying to understand Western European civilization.

In summary, I want to stress that it is not in the

4. See *Japan Quarterly* 8, no. 4 (Oct.–Dec. 1961).

least necessary to go on cherishing the illusions of our Meiji ancestors regarding Western European civilization, namely, the inferiority complex that looked on everything in Western Europe as fine and progressive, and all Japanese things as backward. However, it would create problems if, in reaction, relations between East and West in the future were to be based only on the supposition that the West is amoral. We must study these issues, taking all these factors into consideration.

Translator's note

Japanese Culture is based upon the shorthand record of the public lectures given by the late Professor Ishida in 1965 at Seijō University, Tokyo. The style reflects a presentation for an audience of the general public, and conveys some impression of redundancy since the unexpected death of Professor Ishida prevented a final, thorough revision that would otherwise have been undertaken. For readers with a knowledge of Japanese, the various monographs on Japanese culture in volume 2 of the collected works of Ishida are recommended.

Appendix A:
A CHRONOLOGY OF
JAPANESE HISTORY*

Period	Dates	Events and Major Characteristics
Pre-Jōmon	c. 150,000 B.C.	Pre-ceramic culture; stone implements
Jōmon	c. 7000–250 B.C.	Jōmon pottery culture; hunting and gathering economy
Yayoi	c. 250 B.C.–third century A.D.	Yayoi culture; rice growing; use of bronze and iron
Tomb (Kofun)	Late third to sixth century A.D.	Burial mounds; formation of the Japanese state under the Yamato rulers
Asuka	593–710	Introduction of Buddhism, Confucianism, and religious Taoism; Shinto organized; Chinese influence in law and government
Nara	710–794	Capital at Nara; Buddhist influence on culture
Heian	794–1185	Development of a distinctive Japanese culture; Fujiwara family controls the imperial court in Kyoto
Kamakura	1185–1333	Military rule and evolution of feudalism; Pure Land, Nichiren, and Zen Buddhist sects
Muromachi	1333–1568	Ashikaga shogunate in Kyoto; Zen influence on culture; warring states

* In preparing this chronology I have relied heavily on that in John W. Hall's *Japan: From Prehistory to Modern Times* (New York: Delacorte Press, 1970).

Azuchi-Momoyama	1568–1600	Unification of Japan under Nobunaga, Hideyoshi, and Ieyasu (Tokugawa); introduction of Christianity with the arrival of the first Europeans
Tokugawa (Edo)	1600–1868	Tokugawa family controls government and society; neo-Confucianism; Christianity banned; policy of seclusion
Meiji	1868–1912	End of seclusion; modernization of Japan; Shinto becomes state religion
Taishō	1912–26	Party government; economic and social unrest; mass culture
Shōwa	1926–	Pacific War; American occupation; Shinto disestablished; postwar economic development

Appendix B:
A CHRONOLOGY OF
CHINESE HISTORY*

Dynasty	Dates	Events and Major Characteristics
Hsia	c. 2205–1766 B.C.	Cultivation of wheat and millet; domestication of animals; sericulture
Shang (Yin)	c. 1766–1122 B.C.	Capital established at Yin (Honan province) in 1401 B.C.; use of bronze; written language; oracle bones; ancestor worship
Chou	c. 1112–249 B.C.	Feudal system
Western Chou	c. 1122–771 B.C.	Interstate warfare after invasion of barbarians, 771 B.C.; cavalry; use of iron
Eastern Chou	770–249 B.C.	
Spring and Autumn Annals	722–481 B.C.	Confucius; Lao-tzu; Mencius
Warring States period	403–221 B.C.	
Ch'in	221–207 B.C.	China unified, 221 B.C.; central control; uniform systems of law, language, weights and measures; irrigation works; the Great Wall
Han	202 B.C.–A.D. 220	Confucianism, the state philosophy; Ssu-ma Ch'ien; introduction of Buddhism; defeat of Hsiung-nu; conquest of northern Korea; contact with Japan, first century A.D.

* In preparing this chronology I relied heavily on J. Dun Li's
The Ageless Chinese: A History (New York: Charles Scribner's
Sons, 1965).

Three Kingdoms 220–265 Wei (220–265) Shu (221–265) Wu (222–280)	Warlords
Tsin (Chin) 265–317	Nomadic invasions, early fourth century, drove Tsin south of Yangtze; sixteen states in north China
East Tsin (Chin) 317–420	
Northern and Southern Dynasties 420–589	Invaders Sinicized; Golden Age of Buddhism
Sui 589–618	Block printing; Grand Canal; civil service examinations introduced
T'ang 618–906	Land redistribution; new tax system; conscript army; cultural expansion; conquest of Central Asia and Korea; influence on Japan
Five Dynasties 907–960	Warlordism; foot-binding; printing of Confucian classics
Sung 960–1279	Wang An-shih's reforms, 1069–74
Northern Sung 960–1126	Conquered by nomadic Chin, 1125
Southern Sung 1127–1279	Sung-Chinese rule south of the Yangtze; cultural progress; neo-Confucianism
Yüan 1260–1368	Mongol dynasty; Kublai Khan; disastrous invasions of Japan; Marco Polo
Ming 1368–1644	Naval expeditions; Japanese pirates; Hideyoshi's invasion of Korea; Wang Yang-ming (philosopher)
Ch'ing 1644–1912	Manchu dynasty; Western culture introduced; population increase; peasant uprisings; Western imperialism
Republic 1912–	Manchu dynasty overthrown; republic under Sun Yat-sen; May Fourth Movement; Chiang Kai-shek; Nationalist government
People's Republic 1949–	Chinese Communist Party; Mao Tse-tung; land reform; planned economy

Selected Bibliography

Aida, Yuji. *Prisoner of the British*. Translated by Hide Ishiguro and Louis Allen. London: The Cresset Press, 1966.

Anesaki, Masaharu. *History of Japanese Religion, with Special Reference to the Social and Moral Life of the Nation*. Rutland, Vt.: Charles E. Tuttle, 1963.

——. *Religious Life of the Japanese People*. Revised by Hideo Kishimoto. Tokyo: Kokusai Bunka Shinkōkai, 1961.

Aston, W. G., trans. *Nihongi* [Nihon Shoki]. London: George Allen and Unwin, 1956.

Bellah, Robert N. "Japan's Cultural Identity: Some Reflections on the Work of Watsuji Tetsurō." *Journal of Asian Studies* 24, no. 4 (Aug. 1965).

——. "Shinto and Modernization." In *Continuity and Change: Proceedings of the Second International Conference for Shinto Studies, 1967*. Tokyo: Kokugakuin University, 1968.

——. *Tokugawa Religion: The Values of Pre-Industrial Japan*. Glencoe, Ill.: The Free Press, 1957.

Cooper, Michael, ed. *The Southern Barbarians: The First Europeans in Japan*. Tokyo: Kōdansha International, 1971.

Earhart, H. Byron. *Japanese Religion: Unity and Diversity*. Belmont, Cal.: Dickenson Publishing Co., 1969.

Fukutake, Tadashi. *Japanese Rural Society*. Translated by R. P. Dore. Tokyo: Oxford University Press, 1967.

Groot, Gerald J. *The Prehistory of Japan*. Edited by Bertram S. Kraus. New York: Columbia University Press, 1951.

Herbert, Jean. *Shinto: At the Fountainhead of Japan*. New York: Stein and Day, 1967.

Hilger, M. Inez. *Together with the Ainu: A Vanishing People*. Norman, Okla.: University of Oklahoma Press, 1971.

Holtom, D. C. *Modern Japan and Shinto Nationalism*. Rev. ed. New York: Paragon Book Reprint Corp., 1963.

——. *The National Faith of Japan*. New York: Paragon Book Reprint Corp., 1965.

Hori, Ichiro. "The Appearance of Individual Self-Consciousness in Japanese Religions and Its Historical Transformations." In *The Status of the Individual in East and West*, edited by Charles A. Moore. Honolulu: University of Hawaii Press, 1968.

——. *Folk Religion in Japan: Continuity and Change*. Edited by

Joseph M. Kitagawa and Alan L. Miller. Chicago: University of Chicago Press, 1968.

Inoue, Mitsusada. *Introduction to Japanese History: Before the Meiji Restoration*. Tokyo: Kokusai Bunka Shinkōkai, 1962.

Inoue, Shunji, trans. and annot. *Kojiki*. Fukuoka: Nihon Shūji Kyōiku Renmei, 1958; rev. ed. 1966.

• Ishida, Eiichiro. "A Culture of Love and Hate." *Japan Quarterly* 8, no. 4 (Oct.–Dec. 1961).

• ———. "Japan Rediscovered." *Japan Quarterly* 11, no. 3 (July–Sept. 1964).

———. "Nature of the Problem of Japanese Cultural Origins." In *Japanese Culture: Its Development and Characteristics*, edited by Robert J. Smith and Richard K. Beardsley. Chicago: Aldine Publishing Co., 1962.

———. "Unfinished but Enduring: Yanagita Kunio's Folklore Studies." *Japan Quarterly* 10, no. 1 (Jan.–Mar. 1963).

Kidder, J. E., Jr. *Japan before Buddhism*. New York: Frederick A. Praeger, 1959; rev. ed. 1966.

Kitagawa, Joseph M. *Religion in Japanese History*. New York: Columbia University Press, 1966.

Komatsu, Isao. *The Japanese People: Origins of the People and the Language*. Tokyo: Kokusai Bunka Shinkōkai, 1962.

McFarland, H. Neill. *The Rush Hour of the Gods: A Study of New Religious Movements in Japan*. New York: Macmillan, 1967.

Matsumoto, Shigeru. *Motoori Norinaga, 1730–1801*. Cambridge, Mass.: Harvard University Press, 1970.

Miller, Roy Andrew. *The Japanese Language*. Chicago: University of Chicago Press, 1967.

Miyata, Shimpachirō. "The Father of Japanese Folklore." *Japan Quarterly* 9, no. 4 (Oct.–Dec. 1962).

Muraoka, Tsunetsugu. *Studies in Shinto Thought*. Translated by Delmer M. Brown and James T. Araki. Tokyo: Japanese Government Printing Bureau, 1964.

Nakamura, Hajime. *Ways of Thinking of Eastern Peoples: India, China, Tibet, Japan*. Revised English translation, edited by Philip P. Wiener. Honolulu: East-West Center Press, 1964.

Nakane, Chie. *Japanese Society*. London: Wiedenfeld and Nicholson, 1970.

———. *Kinship and Economic Organization in Rural Japan*. London: University of London Press, 1967.

Norbeck, Edward. *Religion and Society in Modern Japan: Continuity and Change*. Houston, Tex.: Tourmaline Press, 1970.

Ohno, Susumu. *The Origin of the Japanese Language*. Tokyo: Kokusai Bunka Shinkōkai, 1970.

Philippi, Donald L., trans., with an introduction and notes. *Kojiki*. Tokyo: University of Tokyo Press, 1968.

Ross, Floyd H. *Shinto: The Way of Japan*. Boston: Beacon Press, 1965.

Saniel, Josefa M. "The Mobilization of Traditional Values in the Modernization of Japan." In *Religion and Progress in Modern Asia*, edited by Robert N. Bellah. New York: The Free Press, 1965.

Smith, Robert J., and Beardsley, Richard K., eds. *Japanese Culture: Its Development and Characteristics*. Chicago: Aldine Publishing Co., 1962. (Includes papers by Namio Egami, Tadashi Fukutake, Eiichiro Ishida, and Susumu Ohno.)

Takeyama, Michio. *Harp of Burma*. Translated by Howard Hibbett. Rutland, Vt.: Charles E. Tuttle, 1966. (A novel about Japanese soldiers in Burma in World War II.)

Tsunoda, Ryūsaku; DeBary, William Theodore; and Keene, Donald, eds. *Sources of Japanese Tradition*. New York: Columbia University Press, 1958.

Tsurumi, Kazuko. *Social Change and the Individual: Japan before and after Defeat in World War II*. Princeton: Princeton University Press, 1970.

Watsuji, Tetsurō. *A Climate: A Philosophical Study*. Translated by Geoffrey Bownas. Tokyo: Japanese Government Printing Bureau, 1962. Rev. ed.: *Climate and Culture*. Translated by Geoffrey Bownas. Tokyo: Hokuseidō Press, 1971.

Yanagita, Kunio. *About Our Ancestors: The Japanese Family System*. Translated by Fanny Hagin Mayer and Yasuyo Ishiwara. Tokyo: Japan Society for the Promotion of Science, 1970.

Young, John. *The Location of Yamatai: A Case Study in Japanese Historiography, 720–1945*. Baltimore: Johns Hopkins Press, 1958.

Bibliography of Books by Eiichiro Ishida

Kappa komahiki kō 河童駒引考 [A study of the water spirit and its habit of luring horses into the water]. Tokyo: Chikuma Shobō, 1948.

Shinpan. Kappa komahiki kō 新版. 河童駒引考 [New edition. A study of the water spirit and its habit of luring horses into the water]. Tokyo: University of Tokyo Press, 1966.

Issunbōshi 一寸法師 [Legends of Inch Boy]. Tokyo: Kōbundō, 1948.

Momotarō no haha (Issunbōshi kaidai, "Kokubo to kokushin," "Tsuki to fushi," "Tenba no michi," hoka zōho) 桃太郎の母 (『一寸法師』改題,「穀母と穀神」,「月と不死」,「天馬の道」, 他増補) [The mother of Peach Boy (New title for Legends of Inch Boy, with additional essays including "The corn mother and the corn god," "The moon and immortality," and "The road of the celestial horses")]. Tokyo: Hōsei University Press, 1956.

Shinpan. Momotarō no haha 新版. 桃太郎の母 [New edition. The mother of Peach Boy]. Tokyo: Kōdansha, 1966.

Minzokugaku no kihon mondai 民族学の基本問題 [Basic problems in ethnology]. Tokyo: Hokuryūkan, 1950.

Jinrui to bunmei no tanjō 人類と文明の誕生 [The birth of mankind and civilization]. Tokyo: Sanseidō, 1955.

Bunka jinruigaku nōto 文化人類学ノート [Notes on cultural anthropology]. Kawade paperback ed. Tokyo: Kawade Shobō, 1955.

Shinpan. Bunka jinruigaku nōto 新版. 文化人類学ノート [New edition. Notes on cultural anthropology]. Reprints of Famous Books series. Tokyo: Shinsensha, 1967.

Nihon minzoku no kigen 日本民族の起源 [The origins of the Japanese people], in collaboration with Namio Egami, Masao Oka, and Ichirō Yawata. Tokyo: Heibonsha, 1958.

Jinruigaku gaisetsu 人類学概説 [Outlines of anthropology], in collaboration with Kazuo Terada and Eikichi Ishikawa. Tokyo: Nihon Hyōron Shinsha, 1958.

Bunka jinruigaku josetsu 文化人類学序説 [Introduction to cultural anthropology]. Tokyo: Jichōsha, 1959.

Zōtei. Bunka jinruigaku josetsu 増訂. 文化人類学序説 [Revised edition with additional material. Introduction to cultural anthropology]. Tokyo: Jichōsha, 1966.

Jinruigaku 人類学 [Anthropology], in collaboration with Seiichi
   Izumi, Toshihiko Sono, and Kazuo Terada. Tokyo: University of Tokyo Press, 1961.

Tōzai-shō 東西抄 [Essays on East and West]. Tokyo: Chikuma
   Shobō, 1965.

Shinpojium. Nihon kokka no kigen シンポジウム. 日本国家の起源
   [Symposium. The origins of the Japanese state]. Kadokawa
   paperback ed. Tokyo: Kadokawa Shoten, 1966.

Maya bunmei マヤ文明 [The civilization of the Maya]. Chūkō
   paperback ed. Tokyo: Chūō Kōronsha, 1967.

Ningen o motomete 人間を求めて [In search of mankind]. Tokyo:
   Kadokawa Shoten, 1968.

Nihon bunka ron 日本文化論 [Japanese culture: A study of origins
   and characteristics]. Tokyo: Chikuma Shobō, 1969.

Ningen to bunka no tankyū 人間と文化の探求 [Studies of men and
   cultures], anthology. Tokyo: Bungei Shunjūsha, 1970.

Ishida Eiichirō zenshū 石田英一郎全集, 八巻 [Collected works],
   8 vols. Tokyo: Chikuma Shobō, 1970-72.

Index